These B Anglos

GLIMPSES INTO THE ANGLO-INDIAN HEART

HARI BASKARAN

INDIA · SINGAPORE · MALAYSIA

Notion Press

Old No. 38, New No. 6
McNichols Road, Chetpet
Chennai - 600 031

First Published by Notion Press 2018
Copyright © Hari Baskaran 2018
All Rights Reserved.

ISBN 978-1-64249-766-3

Reviews

Let me begin by saying that I love the title of this book on the Anglo-Indian community – These Bloomin' Anglos – which captures the essence of the community, as one that does not take itself seriously, yet attracting the kind of obvious affection and admiration which has led the author to profile the lives of the Anglos he has personally known. Unlike more orthodox studies of the community, his approach is refreshingly different. He opens a window to reveal the everyday lives of people and the unique culture that informs their attitude to life, their successes and failures, their interaction with the community around them, which makes them a beautiful part of the mosaic that is India. The author looks at the community from the outside as a friend and not just a historian. This book will be eminently readable and yet set right as the author aims to do, the stereotypes in literature and film and in popular conception that have distorted the truth about one of India's most significant communities.

I am sure this book will be a valuable addition to the literature on the community.

Dr. Beatrix D'Souza

Former Member of Parliament and former Member, Legislative Assembly (Tamil Nadu) nominated to represent the Anglo-Indian community. Founder President, Forum of Anglo-Indian Women.

A narrative about the Anglo-Indian community written from the heart! Hari Baskaran, in characteristic style, interweaves his discourse with history, memories and personal interactions to present his readers with an account of what it means to be an Anglo-Indian through the eyes of Anglo-Indians as well as from an outsider's perspective that is refreshing both in content and delivery. Informed observations dotted with humour made possible by virtue of having Anglo-Indians in the family and impartial insights as a non-member help deliver a truer account of the community. A suggested read for Anglo-Indian buffs, and if you are from Royapuram, then an enjoyable walk down a memory lane that was once a major Anglo-Indian bastion.

Dr. Cheryl-Ann Shivan,

Principal, Kasthurba College for Women,
A Government of Puducherry Institution,
Villianur, Pondicherry.

The dichotomy in the lifestyles of two cultural groups of people, living and learning within the same vicinity, has taken the prolific author Hari Baskaran down the road of soul-searching nostalgia where he makes informed reflections on the contrasting lifestyles that he witnessed and partially engaged in, in his youth, but whose contradictions had then left him questioning the morals under which he himself was being raised. The book contains interesting vignettes of well-known and lesser-known Anglo-Indians and their families, and by extension, their contributions to India and the countries they have made their homes today, a contribution so very often glossed over by many a non-Anglo-Indian writer in favour of threadbare community stereotypes. The author's interactions with "a broad band of some of the most warm-hearted people you will come across" make interesting reading for it is through these anecdotes that he portrays for his readers the essence of being Anglo-Indian. His reminiscences about Royapuram – an important Anglo-Indian hub of the yesteryears will warm the hearts of its former residences for it takes them down practically every road, every school room and every residence that had an Anglo-Indian presence. The narration, which moves back and forth across time and space, makes effective comparisons between life then and now for the community. A very interesting read for Anglo-Indian enthusiasts, historians and readers of topical interests, delving into the ethos of the Anglo-Indian way of life. The author has made commendable efforts in generating interest in the microscopic but fructifying community.

Dr. Oscar Nigli,

Senior Vice President, All India Anglo-Indian Association,
Tamil Nadu and Pondicherry Branches, Former-MLA,
Tamil Nadu Legislative Assembly and Professor of Economics,
Loyola College, Chennai.

Hari Baskaran's book is a warm, affectionate, nostalgic exploratory into a community that he holds very dear to his heart, and for several good reasons! While delving on the Anglo- Indians we knew and those he met in the course of writing this book, it provides the reader with a wonderful insight into a past that has all but disappeared, in an area of Madras (Chennai).

Growing up among the Anglo-Indians in Royapuram gave him a unique perspective into the lives of a community that has been discriminated and misunderstood for decades due to commonly held mostly negative perceptions.

This appalling perception was largely the result of the British attitude to a community that they created but then felt threatened when the Anglo-Indian culture thrived during their rule. Although the British encouraged the Anglo-Indians to protect their unique culture and social identity, they denied the community the basic right to a British citizenship.

Despite almost insurmountable odds along the way, this microscopic but dynamic community has thrived before, during and after Independence, in India. Their contributions to the homeland in the armed forces, Sports as well as the railways, Health Care, Education are a glorious and lasting tribute to this country.

The community has shrunk considerably over the last few decades due to mass migrations, inter-marriages and natural wastage. Hari laments the fact that our country is poorer due to the exodus, and rightly so!

With reference to the present, the author also goes on to state, and I quote:

"The Anglo-Indian youngsters (of today) know exactly who they are, where they want to be, what it takes to get where they want to go, and to cling passionately and proudly, to their individual images of heaven."

This is the best thing that could happen to this community!

Harry MacLure

Editor, Anglos In The Wind

Contents

Them and Us

When I think of Royapuram, I think of the Anglo-Indians. They were different, although in the impressionable and formative years of my early youth I thought we were different. They were probably the reason for my utter confusion as to what was right and what was wrong, and my sensitive mind kept mulling over this vexing issue often taking me into bouts of solitude and despair.

The Anglo-Indians were a vivacious community, easily giving vent to their feelings and thoughts. We were different; all our emotions were bottled up with a long unwritten list of dos and don'ts. When you are tiny, you do need your space and freedom to express yourself, isn't it? I lived in awe of the Anglo-Indian spirit, but something within me kept asking, *Is this right?* Secretly, I suspected they were but how could I go against the grain of tradition in our households?

Anglo-Indian houses invariably possessed musical instruments such as the guitar and the piano. We believed that this was an unwanted splurge of hard-earned money badly needed for education. The Anglo-Indians loved to express themselves in song; for us, there was simply no need for this form of expression at least in our house, though singing came easily to some of my cousins. As for dancing, the Anglo-Indians were tutored from a very young age, and dance too was an expression of freedom and a means of bringing closeness between the sexes. For us, dance was taboo and closeness of the sexes wasn't the done thing. We were never allowed the slightest show of emotions or feelings even for close cousins. Matronly aunts would hover around making it more than amply clear that we better be prim and proper. Being prim and proper can make you tear your hair in despair; secretly, of course, as you are not expected to do such things in public.

Yet there were clandestine affairs. My maternal great-grandfather, the venerable Choyi, married an Anglo-Indian lady (or a British lady, no one seems to know) and maintained two houses in Kannur; one for my grandmother and family and another for the 'white' side of the family. My brother Gopi, who was stricken with polio, would cycle out most evenings to meet his Anglo-Indian girlfriend and later married a Goan air hostess, Marie D'Gamarose. My brother Ravi married an Anglo-Indian from Royapuram, Marie Rozario. Maybe I didn't play the game of life under my own rules. In those days, I tended to play it by the rules that others had laid down, and I grew to be a harsh critic of myself in the early decades of my life.

My exposure to the Anglo-Indian community started from my early schooling when I studied in Anglo-Indian schools; St. Kevin's, to start with, and then the school I carry so much fondness for, St. Mary's. I grew up in Royapuram, which in those days had a large Anglo-Indian community. My earliest friends from the age of five, Rodney Waples, Brian Jones, Gordon Maitland and others were Anglo-Indians. Cedric Surrao and I studied together from fifth class all the way till we graduated from engineering college. And yet I grew up apart from the Anglo-Indians. I don't remember visiting Anglo-Indian houses and romping around in the Anglo-Indian quarters of Royapuram. I lived and played amidst the Viswanathans, the Chunilals, the Mehtas, the Byramshaws, the Menons and the Georges, hardly ever with the D'Souzas, the Smiths, the D'Costas and the Suarezs.

It is this bond of the past, which had a mix of awe on the one hand and admiration on the other, that led me to write about the Anglo-Indian community. I lost touch with them as I left Royapuram in the early seventies to build a career in the corporate world. My association with the community faded away as I was immersed in my own affairs and the rigours and demands of the corporate world. In their own ways, this was also the case with my Anglo-Indian friends. We were in our respective worlds separated by geography, careers and the choices we made in our lives. The early influences of an Anglo-Indian school upbringing, however, left a deep and indelible imprint on me. For long, the only prayers I offered were 'Abide with Me' and 'Lead Kindly Light,' which I picked up at the moral science classes in school and which remained a part of me for several decades. It was later that I took to the practices of Nichiren Buddhism, which has been my spiritual anchor ever since. I am an English-speaking liberal with a Western cultural orientation thanks to my schooling.

It was during this period of near blackout that most of my Anglo-Indian friends migrated to Australia. Even Cedric vanished from my life without a word, and I met him by chance decades later on a visit to Melbourne. Royapuram, which once had a preponderance of Anglo-Indians, now has only a few families and has changed beyond recognition. Kunhiraman's Stores at the corner of West Mada Church Street is one institution that has remained unchanged over the last half a century. We can still stand on the pavement outside the store and eat mango ice cream and drink grape juice, two favourites of yesteryear, made just as it was 50 years ago.

Over the years, I have sorted out several of the tangled webs in my mind. I am a lot clearer about the desirable way to live one's life. I am a lot more self-assured now though old habits, as they say, die hard. Looking back, I can see that many facets of the Anglo-Indian lifestyle fall into my desirable bucket. I had learnt the essence of life as I plodded along through my life and imbued the life philosophy of Nichiren Buddhism and in the Anglo-Indian community, I saw how intuitively they had adopted this creed and how the sheer joy of living was paramount to their way of life.

Many friends and acquaintances often lampooned the Anglo-Indians and thought of them as a pretty wretched lot. As I researched the community and met several Anglo-Indians, my admiration for them only grew. Their contribution to the country in the armed forces, sports and in basic services such as the railways, healthcare, hospitality, education, etc. was disproportionately high for such a microscopic community. The valour they have shown in the defence of the nation, the devotion to duty and the moral fibre they have demonstrated in the workplace are exemplary. Of course, the community has its own share of rascals, but that does not take away from what is intrinsically good in the community. It is sad that almost two-thirds of them decided to leave the country and settle down in the UK, Canada and Australia. Our country is the poorer because of this mass migration.

The Anglo-Indians live on in India though in much smaller numbers. Their way of life has endured and is prevalent as well as widely spread among the youth of the country. Diversity is well-accepted and today marriages across communities and linguistic barriers are fairly common. The Anglo-Indians are no longer considered different. The Anglo-Indian enclaves of the past that provided havens of differentiation don't exist any longer, and the community has largely integrated into the rest of the country. Yet an Anglo-Indian home still has a different air about it and loads of warmth and friendliness. Community pride still remains even though most other Eurasian communities consider themselves different from the Anglo-Indians and are quick to dissociate themselves from them.

I decided to write this book to showcase, in a small way, glimpses of the warmth, large-heartedness and zest for life that characterises the Anglo-Indian heart. The book touches upon but does not delve into the history of the community at great length. This book looks at the Anglo-Indian heart through the lives of contemporary Anglo-Indians, some who have achieved considerable success in their lives and some just moderate success. In the final analysis, it is the heart that matters. As I reached out to the Anglos, I saw two opposing aspects of their heritage; a regal and affluent creamy layer on the one hand and the undesirable by-products of a mixed race on the other. In between was a broad band of some of the most warm-hearted people you will come across irrespective of their economic status. The book portrays the intrinsic good within a community that is often drowned by commonly held negative perceptions.

As I connected with my erstwhile classmates and Anglo-Indian friends, I received a great deal of encouragement. Many people contributed to the development of this book, but special mention needs to be made of Cedric and Rodney who were instrumental in connecting me with the community in Australia. They and Errol Edmonds, Desmond Holt, Russell Nicholas and Norman Guido offered their time, patience and insights about the community as I spent long hours in discussion with them. Gillean Nash, who married my nephew Bobby Baskaran, her mother Maureen and cousin Ruth Williams were also most helpful and shared their views and memories. Marie Rozario and her family provided a great deal of support during the preparation of this book.

I made several new friends along the way including Tusky Bhaskar, John Castellas, Sharon Newell and Cheryl-Ann Shivan whose interest in Anglo-Indian history and scholarship helped me consider varied perspectives. Barry Peacock, Douglas Simcock, Pat Kerr, Joseph Premkumar and Nikhil Raghavan brought me in touch with a wide cross-section of Anglo-Indians living in India. There are scores of others who also offered assistance in various ways for which I am most thankful.

More than three years have gone into the making of this book, and I have enjoyed every moment of it. I have reconnected with many friends and classmates and made several new friends. The joy and nostalgia of these exchanges have made the preparation of this book a delightful experience. It is dedicated to my many Anglo-Indian friends, old and new, with whom I hope to stay connected as long as I possibly can.

The Anglo Zamindars

Indian military history is replete with European names of brilliant generals and commanders who served the East India Company and the rulers of the princely states. For long, I thought that these worthies were mercenary Europeans who offered their services for financial considerations. It is only after I read more deeply of the accounts of these military heroes that I realised they were Anglo-Indians. In fact, they are the pride of the Anglo-Indian community. The life story of Lt. Col. James Skinner, the founder of Skinner's Horse, which continues to be a regiment of the Indian Army, makes fascinating reading. That I had the good fortune to meet the last surviving male member in India of the Skinner family is another matter.

James Skinner was born to a Scottish father and a Rajput mother. His father had taken a Rajput girl under his protection when he was an ensign with the East India Company. She was the daughter of a zamindar, who bore him six children. James was sent to school and then trained to be a printing apprentice – a role that he disliked and ran away to seek enrolment as a soldier. His mixed parentage denied him entry into either the East Indian Company or the armies of the princely states. Eventually, he was recruited into Maharaja Daulat Rao Scindia's Army and learnt Maratha military tactics over a period of eight years. He quickly rose to command three battalions at the age of 22.

A near-death experience in 1800, while on the battlefield of Uniara (in modern Rajasthan), led him to take an oath that if he lived, he would build a church. St James Church in Kashmiri Gate, Delhi, where Skinner lies buried, is the result of that oath. The church was consecrated on 21st November 1836 and is one of the oldest in Delhi today. A popular account of this experience is that he was shot in the groin and left to die on the battlefield. He spent a harrowing 24 hours grievously wounded till a woman offered him food as well as water and took him to a nearby enemy camp where he was treated well and released after he recovered.

In the 1803 Anglo-Maratha wars, when the Marathas were defeated, Skinner was dismissed from service for being British! He was then offered a commission by the East India Company to raise an irregular horse cavalry. His cavalry was known as the yellow boys on account of the bright yellow tunic and head scarves they wore. The colours reflected a Rajput tradition that as warriors if they could not win, they would die fighting. He gave the cavalry the battle cry: '*Himmat e Mardaan Madad e Khuda*' (God helps the brave) and led them to be a formidable fighting force. His victories in battle resulted in the grants of large tracts of land which besides the properties he purchased made him a large zamindar. He was the landlord of the jagir of Hansi comprising of 194 villages and was always spoken of as a very good landlord.

In a blog- post-dated 14ᵗʰ February 2016, the Indian Defence Review has this to say of James Skinner: "He was fond of delicious Indian food and hookah. He was more comfortable with Persian than English and spoke the local dialect fluently. He knew the names and village of origin of all his men and would often invite men of all ranks to feast with him and lay an old spoon next to his plate to remind him of his humble beginning." The blog-post goes on to say, "After Scindia's defeat in 1803 at Aligarh, 800 men of Perron's Horse offered to join British forces. When they were asked to choose their leader, they unanimously shouted, 'Sikandar Sahib!' and the finest regiment of the Indian cavalry started taking shape."

James Skinner preferred to be referred to by his Moghul title: Nasir-ud-Dowlah Colonel James Skinner Bahadur Ghalib Jung. To the men under his command, he was simply 'Sikander sahib.' He took to scholarship later in life and wrote several books in Persian, among them *Kitab-i tasrih al-aqvam* (History of the Origin and Distinguishing Marks of the Different Castes of India) and another one named *Tazkirat al-Umara*, based on biographies of the Sikh and Rajput princely families and their territories, along with 37 portraits of their existing generation. He was a patron of Moghul painters and took a deep interest in the local people.

James Skinner died in Hansi on 4ᵗʰ December 1841 and was buried with full military honours. Forty days later, his coffin was exhumed and taken with an escort of 200 cavalrymen of the Skinner's Horse to Delhi, where he was buried at St. James Church.

Just after Independence and at the time of the partition, Sikander Sahib's descendants, who were of Muslim, Hindu and Christian faiths, were in a quandary. Eventually, those with allegiance to the Muslim faith went to Pakistan, while many of the others migrated to the UK, Canada and Australia. Only a few remained in India. Today only Lillian Skinner and her brother Jimmy Skinner are alive. That makes Jimmy Skinner the last surviving male descendant of Lt. Col. James Skinner living in India.

I met Jimmy Skinner at an old hunting lodge built by the Powell family, one of the four well-known military families of Anglo-Indian fame. It was well over 100 years old and has been retained almost as it was built with minor modifications. Jennifer Mann, the daughter of Mrs. Doris Powell, lived at the hunting lodge till she passed away in December 2017. The Mann family owns the land and property that once belonged to the Powells.

It was Pat Kerr, son of Lt. General Eric Kerr (Retd.), who arranged a meeting for me with Jennifer and her son Gregory and with Jimmy Skinner. Pat filled me in on the details of the Mann family. "The land owned by the Mann family is in an area which is now called Kunja Grant near Dehradun. It was originally over 300 acres, granted to the Powell family for their services to the Maharaja of Garhwal. After the Zamindari Act most of this land had been taken by the government and about 19 acres are now with the Mann family," he said.

The dried leaves rustled under our feet as we walked along a popular trail on the outskirts of the Rajaji National Park very near

Carbery Acres, a resort owned by the Manns and managed as well as run by Pat. A pack of dogs ran alongside us, happy to have our company. "Jenny is now 76," he said. "She was the pradhan of the surrounding village for nine years. Her son and daughter, Greg and Dolla, run the Carman Schools in Dehradun, while Greg is also the President of the Committee that manages the affairs of the local church and cemetery in Dehradun. He is on the board of several schools in Uttarakhand and is extensively involved with social work." Greg Mann is now the nominated representative of the Anglo-Indian community in the Uttarakhand Legislative Assembly.

Dusk was settling in over Carbery Acres when a staff member ran up to Pat Kerr to say that Dr. Skinner was on his way to meet us. James, or Jimmy as he is called, is tall and of slight build with white hair and dark horn-rimmed spectacles. Being hard of hearing, he wears a large prominent earpiece in his left ear. Pat warned me to speak loudly and also give him the opportunity to lip read as I spoke to him. It was remarkable that at the age of 91, he took so much trouble to meet me as he laboured unaided across the pathway of the resort. He warmly greeted me with a smile and a handshake. Jimmy, I dare say, would bear little resemblance to his great-great-grandfather Sikandar Sahib, who tended to live his life more as a Mughal ruler than an Anglo-Indian. Jimmy, on the other hand, looked quite a genial Anglo-Indian.

It was on Pat's suggestion that we moved to the lodge where we would get to meet Jenny and Greg. Jenny had the early stages of Alzheimer's but was in good spirits throughout our visit, more so when the talk veered around her sharpshooting abilities with a hunting rifle. She has for company her long-standing friend and teaching colleague Dulcie Buttler-White, who was also with us that evening. Jenny has retained a resolute countenance that continues to display a talent for organisation and the ability to get things done; leadership qualities that kept her on as the village pradhani for nine years. She remains well-loved by the neighbouring village communities.

Fig 1. Jenny, Greg and Dulcie White-Butler

There was Glenlivet whisky and Absolut vodka flowing as the modern-day descendants of the Anglo-Indian zamindars of yore entertained us with stories of a forgotten era. Gregory, with his jovial countenance and deep voice, did most of the talking with the elders chipping in from time to time. He vividly described, "In the days gone by the retainers wouldn't allow us to step on to the ground as we alighted from our carriages. They would place a platform for us to get on to and then carry us to the hunting lodge on palanquins." He was referring to the very same hunting lodge where we were seated, which is adjacent to the Carbery Acres Resort.

Between large sips of whisky, Greg said, "The Skinners, the Hersheys and the Powells were some of the well-known military families during the days of the East India Company and the subsequent British rule. These families owned many villages and land in and around the Dehra Dun and Mussoorie areas that were granted to them by the British." His mother Jenny, who now needs the comfort of touch, strokes his hand as he continues, "After the Independence of India, most of the land was taken over by the government post the implementation of the Zamindari Act. The families have retained substantial although small portions of what belonged to them till the present time." Greg walks around the hall as he continues, "Members of the Hershey family eventually sold off their land as well as property and migrated overseas; there are none of them in India. Jimmy Skinner and his sister, Lillian, still take care of the Skinner properties. Mrs. Doris Powell left her land and property to her daughter, Mrs. Carbery, who in turn left it to her two daughters, Jennifer (my mother) and Mauveen Carbery." The property is now owned by Jennifer and the Mann family.

Mussoorie was considered the capital of the heart for the British, unlike Shimla, which was the summer capital and a seat of administration. Mussoorie was used by the British more for leisure, for rest and recuperation and for rehabilitating from illness. The forests around Mussoorie and Dehradun provided wonderful hunting grounds for leisure; a sport that the Anglo-Indian zamindars and their descendants took to along with fishing, till these were banned. Little wonder that hunting and fishing are treasured memories for the Manns and the Skinners.

Jimmy graphically told us how he had shot a deer and Pat added, "Jimmy is a wizard with a hunting rifle." Greg, who was standing just behind his mother Jenny added, "Jenny here shot a leopard with a single shot from a.22 rifle." At my request, the rifle was brought out and both Jenny and Jimmy posed for photographs, rifle in hand. Jimmy brought out several old photo albums and gleefully took me through his favourites, pointing out each time that that was handsome Jimmy! There were several photos of him with catches of large fish, several feet long. He was obviously a keen and enthusiastic angler in his younger days.

Fig 2. Jimmy showing off his treasured photos

It was all about a fascinating lifestyle of opulence. Greg told me how the early Powells brought family retainers, who each had specific duties, to the hunting lodge. First were the Meheras, who were responsible for the upkeep and maintenance of the property; then the Kasayis, who dressed and cooked the meat; then the Gadharias, who tended to the goats, poultry and cattle. They had to ensure sufficient supply of milk and meat for the 'Barra Sahibs' and finally the Bandhookchees (gun bearers), who accompanied them on hunting expeditions and tended to the guns.

Fig 3. A room in the 100-year old hunting lodge

The Mann family represents the upper crust of the Anglo-Indian community. This creamy layer lives across the country these days and has made notable contributions to the country besides working for the welfare of the community and the societies in which they live. The Manns have immersed themselves in socially relevant activities. As a pradhan, Jennifer worked selflessly for the welfare of the village community at Kunja Grant. The school buildings and wells built under her personal supervision continue to be a testimony of her dedication to community service. Gregory continues this tradition as the nominated MLA in Uttarakhand. An achievement he is most proud of is the completion of documentation legalising the ownership, by the church, of the land constituting the burial grounds and in updating as well as maintaining a directory of those buried there and in the proper upkeep of the grounds. He also works tirelessly to assist the aged from all over the state to get their pension as well as medical aid when needed.

Building and repairing broken roads in remote areas and uniting all Christians for the development of the state are his chief concerns. A priority area for him in 2018 is to equip hospitals in the remote areas with badly needed medical equipment. The Manns are highly respected by the local community judging by the reaction of the people I met during my visits to Carbery Acres and the surrounding area and when I sought directions from the policemen at check posts and other bureaucrats.

Greg was very emphatic when he said, "We chose to remain in India because we love the country." Pat echoed this view. Greg's four daughters have also not chosen to migrate. Anglo-Indians across the country have integrated fully with other communities, and it is not surprising to see that one of Greg's daughters has married a non-Anglo-Indian Armoured Corp officer, Ashwin Pundir, whose mother Angella is an Anglo-Indian and is a practising Christian. Jenny's sister Mauveen married an Indian Air Force officer, Wing Commander Ram Khanna and their children have all migrated out of the country. Sadly, Jenny passed away in December 2017 of a heart attack.

From the zamindari opulence, subdued though it may be these days, let's take a look at another aspect of the erstwhile Anglo-Indian lifestyle; the strident efforts to develop a self-sustaining homeland for themselves and the languid lifestyle of the well-to-do pensioners who built homes in this Anglo oasis, albeit in failed projects.

In Pensioners' Paradise

Unlikely as it sounds there was a strident clamour for a homeland by some sections of the Anglo-Indian community. Britain's betrayal of the community and anxiety regarding their fate as the country was inexorably moving towards Independence appeared to have been the driving force for this demand. The best known of the attempts to establish a homeland is McCluskieganj, which was established in 1931. Much has been written about this township, and it has been the inspiration for movie makers and authors to weave their stories. Lesser-known but significant townships for Europeans and Anglo-Indians were established at Whitefield, Bangalore and Clement Town, Dehradun.

I had always thought of Whitefield as the place where a major Sai Baba ashram was located and a way out place that I did not plan a visit to due to its sheer distance from Bangalore. When I came to know that it was once an Anglo-Indian settlement, I took the first available opportunity to make a visit there and meet some of the long-standing residents; folks who have been witness to the changing times in what was once a land of hope for the Anglos who wanted desperately to protect their identity. Alas, Whitefield also suffered the fate of other Anglo-Indian enclaves as the community migrated leaving behind just a handful of families and the march of 'progress' blanked out the original intent of the township.

In the period when the East India Company was expanding its influence across the country, they deemed it necessary to create a bulwark that would serve their military and administrative interests, with a community that would be loyal to them and an ideal bridge with the native Indian population. A sum equivalent to five rupees was paid for every child born to a British subject and a native woman. All through the rise of the East India Company the children of these mixed marriages, our very own Anglos, were treated without any discrimination and were given preference in military service and in administrative positions in public utility services. Anglo-Indians were allowed to go to England for higher education if their fathers could afford it, opening the way for them to take on senior supervisory positions. This was a golden period of prosperity for the Anglo-Indians. By 1750, the Anglo-Indians outnumbered the British in India and were truly a bulwark for the East India Company. In the words of Herbert Stark, "The bulk of the fighting fell on the Anglo-Indians. But for them, the French would have expelled the British from India." (Frank Antony – *The Story of the Anglo-Indian Community*). Military background and training is part of the Anglo-Indian heritage.

The first betrayal, as Frank Anthony says, was when the shareholders of East India Company felt that it was unwise to allow the Anglo-Indians unfettered access to power and position as they may one day turn against them. The perceived threat, submitted in a report to the shareholders of the company was, "In every country where this intermediate caste has been permitted to rise, it has ultimately tended to its ruin. Spanish-America and San Domingo are examples of this—it may justly be apprehended that this tribe may hereafter become too powerful for control." (Frank Anthony – *The Story of the Anglo-Indian Community*). The direct consequence of this apprehension was that an order was passed in 1795 baring Anglo-Indians from military service and also all but clerical positions in the civil services. Anglo-Indians in the military were discharged from service and given only non-combatant roles.

Just prior to Independence, Britain made it clear to the leaders of the Anglo-Indian community that they were an integral part of the Indian nation with a right to protect their own culture and social identity. They had no intention to allow a race that they had assiduously created the right to British citizenship. The Anglo-Indians under the leadership of Lt. Col. Sir Henry Gidney, and later under Frank Anthony, battled hard to ensure recognition of Anglo-Indians as a minority community with representation in the legislative assembly and reservations in services such as railways, Post and Telegraphs and Customs. The Anglo-Indians remained anxious about their future amidst the growing nationalism in the country. They felt alienated and perceived a threat to their culture and way of life. A homeland for Anglo-Indians, however, seemed an unlikely solution to their concerns. Nevertheless, persistent efforts were made to achieve this end.

Timothy McCluskie, an Anglo-Indian businessman from Kolkata, was able to convince the Raja of Ratu in Chota Nagpur to provide 10,000 acres of land for establishing a homeland for people with a European lineage. This land was at Lapra, approximately 62 kilometres from Ranchi and located next to the Lapra railway station. McCluskie formed a company called the Colonisation Society of India for the purpose of forming a community of landowners in his proposed township. The township was named McCluskieganj after he passed away in 1935. Anglo-Indians who purchased a share in this society were granted a plot of land for building a house and for farming. McCluskie's marketing skills helped attract 350 families to settle in the new township.

As Malcolm Hourigan, one of just a handful of Anglo-Indians left in the township, says, "The Anglo-Indians came to this wilderness and built their Anglican bungalows with flower gardens and tiled slanted roofs. They built two churches, a club, an abattoir, a post office, poultry farms and horse stables. They brought their pianos, their heavy wooden chests, their riding breeches, their rifles and shotguns, their chatter, their party gowns, lace curtains, rum cakes and beer." (Malcolm Hourigan in *Holding on: The Anglo-Indian Settlement in McCluskieganj*) Hourigan attributes the migration out of the township to the lack of revenue generating opportunities and also as most of the settlers were retired folk without experience in doing business or farming, they found the going tough. "The fate of McCluskieganj fell prey to an experiment that had not factored in the economic variables," he went on to say.

There are moves to keep McCluskieganj going as in 1997 an English medium school, Don Bosco Academy, was established and this attracted a large number of students from across Bihar and Jharkhand. As the school has no hostel facilities (apparently a deliberate ploy), a new avenue for financial gain has arisen as the residents set up hostels and secured jobs as teachers. Recently, the Government of Jharkhand has designated the township as a tourist site, which is likely to bring in funding and additional infrastructure. The few Anglo-Indians who live there, however, are tired of being interviewed and written about as the remnants of a bygone era.

The Eurasian and Anglo-Indian settlement of Whitefield was founded on 27 April 1882, when the Maharaja of Mysore State granted 3,900 acres to the Eurasian and Anglo-Indian Association, Mysore and Coorg, for the establishment of agricultural settlements at Whitefield. It got its name from the President of the Association, DS White, who took a great deal of interest in its development. In the first decade of the 1900s, there were about 45 houses and 130 residents. Whitefield was connected by train and buses to Bangalore about 20 kilometres away. Reaching the settlement from the Whitefield railway station was possible only by writing a letter to Mrs. Hamilton (wife of James Hamilton, the keeper of the Waverly Inn), who would arrange for a bullock cart trip for eight annas!

Douglas Simcock, a 1965 war veteran, set up a memorable meeting for me in June 2017, with Merlyn D'Souza, her son Paul and Christa Moss, long-standing and well-known residents of Whitefield. A ring of chairs, in the courtyard of a 100-year-old house, in the shade of tall trees with a cool breeze rustling through the leaves and the sun making shifting patterns on the ground took us away from the hustle and bustle of modern-day Whitefield to a time several decades ago. The setting was idyllic.

Fig 4. Paul, Douglas, Christa and Merlyn at "Perfect Peace."

Paul and Merlyn's house is over 100 years old and has been retained largely as it was, except for an extension that the previous owners had carried out about 30 years ago. This is just one of a few heritage houses that remain in Whitefield. The D'Souza family bought the house from Leslie John Rourke in June 1988; a house they had set their mind on. In gratitude for the Rourke's refusing more lucrative offers for the house, they insisted that the elderly couple stay on in a wing of the house rather than move to an old age home. Merlyn said, "Paul took great care of Leslie. He would change his diapers and care for him when he was unwell." Visitors to the bungalow say that they sense peace and calm even as they walked down the pathway from the gate to the front porch. "I felt it too from the very first moment," said Merlyn. She went on to name the house 'Perfect Peace.'

Merlyn arranged the setting for the meeting reminiscent of the leisure morning meetings that were a common practice in Whitefield, a place often referred to as the original pensioners' paradise and the preferred location to settle for pensioners from Kolar Gold Fields (KGF), Bangalore, Mysore and Madras. Merlyn said, "The maids would cook lunch and lay the table neatly with the best of crockery, cutlery and napkins before they leave. Eurasian and Anglo-Indian friends walked in and out of each other's houses sitting around and discussing the gentle social ripples of the day and engaging in leisure chatter."

Amidst the animated conversation, Merlyn served homemade brownies, cakes and an Anglo-Indian favourite, mango fool; a drink made of crushed mangoes, milk and a dash of lime, from mangoes that grew in their garden. The snacks were served in impeccable style on elegant quarter plates and with well-pressed red napkins. The D'Souzas are conservationists at heart. The leaves that copiously fall in spring are swept to a corner of the garden where they disintegrate naturally and are spread back into the soil. There is no burning of leaves or disposal as garbage.

Christa, now in her eighties, still moves around on a cycle and walks briskly. She retains a positive and cheerful disposition to life. She experienced the lifestyle of the early days in Whitefield when horses and bullock carts were the modes of transport and everybody knew each other. Maids and vendors were the vehicles to pass on messages between houses. She watched with alarm, tinged with resignation, as the high-rise culture took over. Happiness in life does not come from the sole intent of material gain, power or position. The 12th-century Buddhist monk Nichiren says, "More valuable than the treasures of the storehouse are the treasures of the body, and the most valuable of all are the treasures of the heart." The pursuit of the treasures of the heart leads people to work not just for their own happiness but the happiness of other people.

Here are a few snatches from an excellent and moving poem composed by Christa as the changing times wrenched her heart:

In springtime nineteen seventy-eight
Whitefield hadn't grown that much,
Still had a distinctive rural touch.
Till exuding peace and calm

It hadn't lost its old-world charm.

I miss the ragi fields next door.

I don't hear the crickets anymore.

The chorus of frogs is a thing of the past.

I don't even know when I heard it last.

Progress has put a stop to all that,

Developers have grown very fat.

The last ten years saw the fastest change,

The unimaginable range

Of high-rise blocks crowding the sky.

No wonder it is losing its soul,

The settlers who made the first small waves

Must be turning in their graves.

Just as Christa has no intention of leaving Whitefield, Douglas also sees no reason to leave although his daughter has migrated to the UK. Merlyn doesn't wish to leave either though she said, "I wanted Paul to go to Australia and build a career as he has been tied to the house looking after the elderly Rourkes." Paul, however, adds, "I went to Australia for four months but decided not to migrate there as my workaround inventions are better served in India." Like many Anglo-Indians who have siblings or children settled abroad, these folks are emotionally bound to the country and prefer to live in India with all its imperfections.

Fig 5. The wishing well

Perfect Peace is an Anglo-Indian house of the past. The D'Souzas have retained its original character. Each piece of furniture reflects the vintage nature of the house. Merlyn said, "Every piece of furniture has been carefully chosen and holds a great deal of memories for us." Paul has a penchant for old clocks and the room he calls his quarters has several ancient clocks on the walls and in ancient cupboards. There are little touches around the house and its spacious garden that reflects the D'Souzas' love for the quaint. At the corner of the garden is a beautiful wishing well. Paul, an innovator and a handyman, constructed it in response to Merlyn's desire to have one when the Rourkes were unwell and needed the good wishes of everyone.

Fig 6. Paul's quarters with the antique clocks

The establishment of an IT Park in Whitefield has resulted in a buzz of traffic. Whitefield Main Road is now so busy it could take half an hour to cross the road during peak hours. With several multinational firms setting up offices, real estate prices have skyrocketed. Whitefield is no longer the quaint Anglo-Indian settlement of old and the lazy, languid lifestyle is a thing of the past.

The primary purpose for Anglo-Indian settlements such as McCluskieganj and Whitefield may no longer be relevant and the character of the settlements all but decimated. However, they represent the pioneering spirit of the Anglo-Indian community; the heritage of a rare breed of people and their desperate attempts to retain their cultural identity. It is sad that little or no efforts are being taken to preserve this heritage.

My journey to the discovery of the Anglo-Indians took me to an understanding of the military background that runs in the blood of the community and the pioneering zeal that sought to build a separate and self-sustaining homeland to protect their culture and social identity. It's time to visit the prejudices that dogged the community even as they held their heads high with the pride of service and achievements.

Prejudice and Pride

For those who like to cock a snook at the Anglo-Indians, here are a few eye-openers when you consider their contribution to the national pride. The Indian hockey team that won the 1928 Olympic gold medal had eight Anglo-Indians in the team. In the mid-fifties and sixties, at least two of the Pierce brothers represented the Australia hockey team at the Olympics. Wilson Jones was the Indian Billiards champion for 12 years. He became the first Indian world sporting champion when he won the World Billiard Championship in 1958 and regained the title in 1964. Kenneth Powell won 19 national sprinting titles during a seven-year period from 1962 to 1967.

During the construction of the first railway line by the Great Indian Peninsular Railway in 1851, 3000 Anglo-Indians worked on the project as foremen, supervisors, technical personnel and clerical staff. Anglo-Indian military prowess resulted in the formation of legendary military units which have continued in the Indian Army even today. They include, not exhaustively, Skinner's Horse founded by Lt. Col. James Skinner and the Shekhawati Brigade, later known as the 13th Rajput Regiment, formed by Col. Henry Forster. In more recent times, post-independence and going on into the fifties, more than 50% of the pilots in the Indian Air Force were Anglo-

Indians. As many as eight Anglo-Indians reached the rank of Air Vice Marshall (at last count). Air Chief Marshall Denis Fontaine went on to head the Air Force while Admiral Pereira headed the Indian Navy. Major General Henderson-Brooks, the first Anglo-Indian to be made Major General, was assigned the task of inquiring into the 1962 debacle in the conflict against China.

Views on the Anglo-Indians of yore expressed by almost everyone is that this is a dynamic and fun-loving community and they hold fond memories of friends and admiration for their way of life. Sailendra (Tusky) Bhaskar, a past student of St. George's Homes, Ketti, says, "During my school days I thought of Anglo-Indians, barring exceptions, as a trifle below par but later as I researched the community in depth and also had occasion to meet many who had settled down well in their careers, I developed a great deal of admiration for the community."

Anglo-Indians were generally accepted to be apolitical, good team players and diligent at work. Anglo-Indian girls were for long considered the most efficient and dependable secretaries and easily the best-looking air hostesses. The literature on the community, even in the post-Independence era, is replete with stories of members of the community who have fought valiantly for the country and have risen to the highest ranks in various walks of life.

Air Chief Marshal Denis La Fontaine, Admiral Ronald Pereira, Lt. General Reginald Naronha, the Keelor brothers, Eric Stracey (former Director-General of Police in Tamil Nadu), Ruskin Bond (one of India's best storytellers), Melville de Mello (the voice of All India Radio), Olympian Leslie Claudius, Wilson Jones (the country's first world champion), Frank Anthony, Derek O'Brien, and the list can go on and on, are Anglo-Indians who did their community proud and are household names in India.

I will surely be guilty of several prominent omissions in this list of glory and honour. The aim was not to create an exhaustive list. A little peek into the achievements of the community is enough to conclude that Anglo-Indian contribution to national achievements far exceeds the community's microscopic size. It is reports of this nature that make one sit up and ask what it is that makes this community tick and contrast it with the widely held unflattering perceptions of the community.

Being labelled a 'mixed race' has led to certain sections of the population stereotyping Anglo-Indians as undesirable and a by-product of illegitimate union with British soldiers. In a country colonised for so many centuries, mixed races are natural. The policies of the East India Company, and also for that matter the Portuguese, created a distinct population that had the sanction of the colonisers. It is well documented that the colonisers encouraged liaisons and marriages between their subjects and the local women and even paid an allowance for children of such unions. Large numbers of such liaisons led to abandonment and destitution and to their assimilation into other communities.

Cheryl-Ann Shivan is quite emphatic when she says that anyone who wishes to understand the Anglo-Indian community must read the historical context that led to the community's plight. She refers to the betrayal of the community by the British and draws attention to several books on the subject, notably, *These are the Anglo-Indians* by Reginald Maher and *Hostages to India* by H.A. Stark.

The Anglo-Indian community is a complex matrix of people of different 'stock' and the implicit social stratification. At one end are the offspring of the wedlock between the Europeans holding administrative positions and domiciled in India and Indians or Anglo-Indians and at the other end are the descendants of those from the lower hierarchy of the railways and the armed forces. Lord Olivier says that persons of mixed blood are potentially the most competent vehicles of humanity. He, however, qualifies this assertion when he says, "It depends on what level and at what stage of civilisation the mixture takes place. If the offspring is the product of a low-class British Tommy and a servant woman, the result is not likely to be a competent vehicle of humanity. But when the intermarriage has been at middle-class or at upper-middle class level, the offspring have more than held their own with the finest types of so-called unmixed races, white or brown." (Frank Anthony – *The story of the Anglo-Indian Community*)

It would be unfair if we make sweeping comments about the community based on observations of the lower strata. As Frank Anthony said, "Peripatetic writers in search of lurid details and cheap sensationalism usually hit upon the lowest specimens in the community." Two excellent books, *The Anglo-Indians: A 500-year history* by S Muthiah and Harry MacLure and *Britain's Betrayal in India: The story of the Anglo-Indian community* by Frank Anthony delve into the history of the community and is a must-read for anyone who wishes to get a deeper insight into the origins of the community.

In the Malabar region of Kerala, there are hushed mentions of the 'white stain' – the liaisons between the women of certain communities and the British. These liaisons have generally been quietly accepted, and as a result, there is a large admixture of European blood and people of fair complexion in that part of Kerala. The offspring of these liaisons are fully integrated with the rest of the community and in that sense, have disappeared. Their integration and acceptance within the community have limited the prejudices against them.

Mixed races of this nature tend to disappear over time but for the Anglo-Indians, a stubborn adherence to their British heritage, remaining almost strictly endogamous, and adherence to a Western lifestyle and dresses have kept them apart as a distinct entity for 500 years and more. Frank Anthony writes, "Marriages were jealously confined within the walls of the community. It was regarded as social anathema to marry even a light-skinned, most highly placed member of another community in preference to an ebony-hued, poor Anglo-Indian."

The Western-style dresses of Anglo-Indian girls were a source of prejudice in the 20th century and the dawn of the 21st. Bollywood movies cast the vamps in Western dresses and the demure heroines in saris, leading to deep-rooted prejudices against the sinful Western-style dressing. Muthiah says, "Virtually every home has a tradition of popular Western and church song and music, many own a piano and today's youth favour guitars and harmonicas. A corollary is learning Western (ballroom) dancing from a young age; foxtrots, waltzes and jives are the favoured forms. This, together with a more informal relationship with parents, has long led to an ease in conversation and a greater intermingling of the sexes. In conservative Indian eyes, the enjoyment of song and dance has long been seen as promiscuity in the women and a lack of serious focus in the men."

Times have changed and one can witness in the India of today, in almost all middle-class and upper middle-class urban homes, this easy informality in conversation between the parents and children and free intermingling of the sexes. The Western-style of dressing is very common; in fact, it is the preferred mode of dressing among the young girls of all communities in India, and the informed public sentiment is that women have the right to dress as they feel comfortable besides having the right to self-expression. That's the style, ladies! For their part, Anglo-Indian ladies often dress in saris and salwars besides their Western-style dresses and are indistinguishable from the ladies of other communities.

The Anglo-Indians have their own class divide mainly on economic lines, but there is a subtle divide on the basis of what some call the 'purity' of the line, a consideration of being more British than others of their community. This often got translated into the class distinction of the fairer sections of the community from their darker skinned brethren. Cedric Dover calls it 'the urge for purity among the impure.'

Norman Guido, the well-known plastic surgeon and artist, told me that his mother was East Indian and his wife's mother was also East Indian. They see themselves as distinct from Anglo-Indians although the distinction is not quite so apparent. I remember the night when a group of carol singers came to Norman's house. On enquiring if they were Anglo-Indians, the quick response was that they were Mangalorians and Goans and a more well-to-do group. There is a class distinction emerging in such statements by Mangalorians and Goans who are very quick to dismiss any association with the Anglos. By the same token, the reference groups for Anglo-Indians these days seem to be the Mangalorians and Goans.

The Anglo-Indians were ridiculed over what was considered their belief in being more British than Indian and yet being shunned by the British. Those who wish to take a swipe at the community refer to their manner of speaking: the cockney element, the frequent use of 'man,' the dropping of 'H,' the bugger offs, the bloodies, the oft-used one-liners and so on. Our school teachers, most of them Anglo-Indians, took pains to speak the best of English; we learnt our English from them. It is difficult to imagine them slipping into Anglo-Indianisms.

In less formal surroundings they may well have thrown in a few bugger offs and one-liners just as we often did. Anglo-Indians speak this way informally, in small groups, when they let their hair down and slip in the bloody this and the bloody thats or make references to 'the Indian buggers.' I've got to say I do use 'bugger off' from time to time. I quite like using the term when talking to close friends.

Anglo-Indians are quite happy to have a dig at their mannerism and there are several video clips on YouTube by Anglo-Indians taking a little bash at themselves. John Casteles sent me a delightful titbit which I have partially reproduced.

Way back in the 70s, Jeffry and Aather were 'aving an argment, chile. Over 'oo went off back 'ome to Englan afterr the bledgy war, men. Dey agreed to disagree bout oo went and oo stayed, but I know ow it 'appened. See chile, all d'anglos were given a choice by de Indian guvment. Go off 'ome, or stay 'ere an live with the bledgy locals. Dat time, the Peters, der Thompsons, the Burbys, der Moores an der Kirkbys all went off to live with dare kith and kin back 'ome. All the duffers like us, din go.

The Anglos today don't generally carry any baggage of the early postcolonial days.

My mother harboured stereotypical prejudices against the community but considered my childhood friends Brian, Rodney and Cedric atypical of the community at large and more acceptable. Besides, they were boys! This was strange as my great-grandfather, my mother's grandfather, married twice;

the first wife being my great-grandmother and the second, an Anglo-Indian or a British lady.

For long, the children of the second marriage were forbidden from entering my great-grandmother's ancestral home in Kannur, Kerala. The 'white' side of the family lived in another beautiful home called 'the Gardens.' After my great-grandfather's death, there was a reconciliation, and both sides of the family lived in harmony. Over time there were several inter-marriages between the extended families of the two sides. Perhaps my mother's views of the community came from those early prejudices against the white community. However, over time, there was a clear acceptance that the children of the white side of the family performed very well in life, reaching positions of stature in various walks of life. There was grudging admiration for them, and my mother and others on her side of the family maintained very friendly relations with the other side.

Notwithstanding displays of prejudice, my mother accepted the marriage of two sons to Eurasians with grace and dignity. Ravi married Marie Rosario, an Anglo-Indian, and Gopi, Marie D'Gamarose, a Goan. While Gopi lived a very independent life in distant Mumbai, my mother lived with Ravi and Marie and had to make adjustments as well as accept differences in cultural and religious sentiments. My brother's three children were baptised as Catholics in Mata Dolorosa Church and had strong leanings to their Anglo-Indian roots and yet, as Marie says, they had the best of both worlds; they celebrated Christmas and Easter, sang and danced freely and also participated in the Vishu and Onam festivities. Ravi's daughter Sandhya's marriage was in a church, but she insisted on having the Malayali custom of the bride dressed in a traditional sari, sitting before prayer lamps and being blessed by the elders of the family on the day before the marriage. It was a custom she had seen at other family weddings that had struck a chord in her heart.

Fig 7. Sandhya receiving blessings before her marriage

Marie would say to her friends, "It just did not matter that I belonged to a different community, religion or culture. I was welcomed and accepted wholeheartedly at Hartland (the Baskaran's family home). Ravi's family joined in Christmas celebrations, parties, etc., and I used to help my mother-in-law make artistic carpets for Onam. My parents would visit Hartland and view the Vishu 'Kani' and receive silver coins and 'nei appams' from my mother-in-law."

We sold Hartland after my mother passed away. Ravi and Marie moved to Aminjikaria, Chennai, and their home took on the unmistakable look of a Catholic home with images of Jesus Christ and the Cross prominently displayed. My brother Ravi had no objection to this. In fact, in his later days, he would from time to time go to church along with Marie. He said the church provided him with a lot of peace and calm. When he passed away, a victim of cancer, in February 2014, Marie was in a quandary as to how his funeral ceremony needed to be conducted. Our family told her that it would be best and appropriate if she conducted the last rites in the Catholic tradition. A service was held for my brother at the nearby church and he was buried at a cemetery in Washermanpet where many Anglo-Indians of Royapuram, including Marie's parents, were buried.

Anglo-Indians of that period were rarely given to higher education beyond high school; a hangover from the days of almost guaranteed employment in services such as the railways, Post and Telegraphs and the Police. Some Anglo-Indians say the Anglo-Indians are lazy 'buggers.' Sharon Newell brings out a different perspective. We, in India, place an overwhelming emphasis on education that leads to supervisory jobs and we have a disdainful view of skills training. Skills, on the other hand, are rewarded with high wages in Australia and other Western countries. It is unfortunate that those in India who equip themselves with skills are thought of as blue collared and inferior and even unsuitable for the supervisory cadres. With Anglo-Indians of that era predominantly taking on skill-based jobs, it is not surprising they were victims of this disdain.

We all hold our own prejudices and paradigms and I was guilty of an indulgence when speaking to a young lady from Punjab on a flight from Singapore to Melbourne. Her speech, accent and general deportment got me to presume her husband, whom she was joining in Melbourne, was an IT professional but was taken aback when she said he was a tram driver. How vain we are! The lady had a mature and balanced view of life and immediately told me, "Tram and taxi drivers are looked down upon in India, but they are not in Australia. My husband is quite happy living as a tram driver in a place where there is dignity of labour."

The key to happiness and contentment is not in status and position but in an attitude and a behaviour that is insular from rank, title and position. Much as this is easy to accept, it generally takes a long time before this deep-rooted motivator withers away. The roots lie dormant in the recesses of the mind and sometimes sprout again like hardy scrubs. The Anglo-Indians have an intrinsic awareness of the essence of joyful living; theirs was a more 'evolved' state of life. There is much to learn from the Anglo-Indian way of life.

Anglo-Indians tended to be most comfortable in their own little groups. This was noticeable at mixed community gatherings such as at colleges, hostels, etc. They stuck together in their little comfort zones. All this changed over time as the number of Anglo-Indians dwindled post the migration waves in the mid-sixties, seventies and eighties and the community sought greater integration with the rest. Mixed marriages also enabled this integration as did clothing and language. It is difficult to see today in India, the Anglo-Indians of old.

Shyam Sunder, of the well-known band 'Shyam and the West Winds,' is Anglo-Indian in his upbringing as well as his love for music, and for a laugh, he can switch to the typical Anglo-Indian mode of speech. Shyam approached the Anglo-Indian Association in Bangalore, probably in jest, to consider him an Anglo-Indian on the basis of a European lineage somewhere in the past. This was not accepted as can be expected! He may not have had conclusive evidence of the European lineage, or because he was not a Christian or just because such a request was unprecedented. Shyam could easily pass off as an Anglo-Indian any day.

Norah Augustus, George Philipsz and Bonaventure Maria Lawrence, whom I met over lunch at the Catholic Club in Bangalore, miss the Anglo-Indian way of life as we knew it in the sixties and seventies. There is, however, a latent desire to retain and give expression to the old way of life; the fun and gaiety, the dance and music and the bonhomie when friends get together. The vibrancy of old comes out in the New Year's Eve dances and May Queen Balls conducted at the Catholic Club. There is a sense of pride here.

Anglo-Indians who migrated to Australia have by and large done very well for themselves. "Anglo-Indians are stable, conscientious workers, with extended family networks and a lively social life. They remained interested in India and the East, showing concern for Anglo-Indians still in India. Their settlement has been generally smooth and trouble-free, and they maintain good relations with other groups." (Dr. Gloria J Moore – *A Brief History of the Anglo-Indians*). They have houses of their own, cars and all basic necessities and most importantly, their children have been educated and are doing well; in most cases, better than their parents could ever have hoped to be. Many Anglo-Indians have taken to entrepreneurship and built lucrative businesses, a trait they had little opportunity to show in India in the era when they chose to migrate. The situation in India is very different now as Anglo-Indian entrepreneurs I met said that they had been to the UK and Australia for extended periods of three to six months before deciding that India was the place where they could best develop their business interests.

The cynicism and derision that one witnessed in the days of old towards Anglo-Indians is almost absent today. It is almost as if the community didn't exist or is irrelevant. The Parsees, the Coorgis and even the Goans continue to have a distinct identity of their own and more than a little positive acceptance. Anglo-Indians, for the sake of economic progress, have tended to integrate with the other communities through marriage, language and customs. As Muthiah says in his book, "They're Indians today, whose community is Anglo-Indian, religion Christianity and language English." Quoting further from Muthiah's book, *Anglo-Indians: A 500-year history*, Derek O'Brien said, "India has a glorious tomorrow; the Anglo-Indian community must be part of that tomorrow." He was echoing Frank Anthony: "Let us always remember that we are Indians. The community is Indian. It has always been Indian. Above all, it has an inalienable Indian birthright."

A seminar titled 'Anglo-Indian youth – The Renaissance' that was held in January 2017 in Chennai brought out the vibrancy and dynamism of today's young Anglo-Indians. The seminar was sponsored by Blair Williams and organised by The Forum of Anglo-Indian Women. Bryan Oliver Peppin had this to say of the youth who participated in the seminar, "There were college students more eloquent than some of their teachers, young professionals who took great pride in their work and their achievements, entrepreneurs who were doing handsomely in their chosen fields… this was a new generation, a new breed of Anglo-Indians who were willing to take on the world and who were succeeding." He went on to say, "These Anglo-Indian youngsters knew exactly who they were, where they want to be, what it takes to get where they want to go, and to cling passionately and proudly, to their individual images of heaven." –*Anglos in the Wind*, March 2017.

This is the best thing that could happen to this community.

A Tryst with Friends from the Past

For several decades I had lost contact with my dear friends from school. I never really questioned why they had chosen to migrate out of the country. I missed them and hoped we would reconnect some day; the digitally connected world brought us closer together in recent times. Meeting them at their homes in Melbourne and re-establishing the ties of old was very emotionally satisfying. For the Anglos who chose to migrate the choice was between merging with the other communities in India and merging with the more acceptable English-speaking, Christian lifestyle of the Australians. It was a no-brainer for the Anglos who had a ready propensity to leave the country.

Australian immigration policy, however, was fraught with racism till the mid-sixties. The 'white Australian' policy in specific terms bared Anglo-Indians from migrating to Australia unless they had a predominant European parentage, a Western lifestyle and fair skin. "The Department of Immigration was unambiguous in its desire to restrict the entry of Anglo-Indians and stated that persons of mixed blood coming from tropical countries do not, on the whole, prove a very desirable type of migrant and Australia would suffer no loss if the conditions governing their entry were to further limit the numbers admitted." (Alison Blunt – *Postcolonial migration: Anglo-Indians in 'White Australia'*) By the mid-sixties, the immigration policy was modified to accept migrants of mixed blood if cultural affinity could be demonstrated on the basis of appearance, education, upbringing, outlook, mode of dress and way of living and not on appearance or colour only. This led to a near exodus of Anglo-Indians to Australia. However, as Alison Blunt says, "Anglo-Indians could migrate to Australia from the late 1960s because they were seen as culturally European, but when they arrived they were often perceived as Indian. Many Anglo-Indians suffered racial prejudice."

It was against this backdrop that I set off to Australia to meet my boyhood Anglo-Indian friends to re-establish contact with them and re-kindle the magical moments of our childhood. I was completely non-judgemental. I was quite sure that most of them had come out reasonably successful and had little to complain of in terms of their financial situation, quality of life and the opportunities that they provided to their children to live a life far in excess of their own. The decisions they made were entirely of their own choosing and if it worked out well for them, so be it. It was in the autumn

of 2016 when the long summer spell had eased into chilly
weather that I reached Melbourne.

Fig 8. Buddies meet after a long time

Cedric Surrao, the ever reliable, was at the airport to meet me
and we were soon motoring along the Tullamarine highway
to his house in Wantirna, an eastern suburb of Melbourne.
Cedric has been one of my closest friends all these years.
He hasn't changed much over the years but for greying. He
is slimly built and a touch short in stature, but he has an
enormously large heart. I always wondered why Cedric chose
to migrate out of the country. He had told me that he lost his
heart to the girl he married after a courtship of a few months.
It all clicked at the first meeting, he had said. I was dumb-
founded.

Fig 9. Cedric and family

We drove into Cedric's house and were greeted by Sheryl, his wife, who made such an upheaval in his life. I sank into a comfortable sofa as Sheryl rustled up a cup of green tea for Cedric and me. There is warmth and cosiness about Cedric's house with its lace curtains and pastel upholstery. The Surraos have been living here for over 40 years. Several Anglos have tended to move to bigger houses as their financial situation improved. Cedric said, "We never felt the need to shift to another bigger place. Now, many others are moving from larger houses to smaller ones as it is easier to maintain."

Fig 10. Sheryl and Cedric

"When did you migrate to Australia, Cedric?" I asked. "In 1981," he replied. Cedric is not given to open displays of emotion, so he communicates his thoughts in a matter of fact manner. He inherited his taciturn nature from his dad and composure from his mother. Cedric had the best of both worlds; the world of the Anglos and the world of the Indians. "Did your engineering education and experience at Carborundum Universal count for anything?" I asked. "No, it was tough going. I had to start from the very bottom," he said in a resigned manner. It was just like Cedric to let his heart rule his decisions.

I asked myself if I would ever consider giving up everything and starting from the bottom of the ladder in another country and the answer was, "Hell no way." Perhaps I value social recognition and position. This is a tendency that lingers deeply in my mind, and I dare say in a lot of us, and drives decision making. Relocating to another country such as Australia may not have given me the opportunity to live life to the full in ways more conducive than my own country. *Why the hell would I consider migration?* I thought to myself. Cedric, however, has this happy ability to live life with a mind free of clutter, a commendable trait that comes naturally to Anglo-Indians.

The Surraos are a large family of eight siblings who lived in Royapuram with their parents in a rather cramped house on West Mada Church Street. All the Surrao brothers migrated by the year 2000. It took Denzel ten years after the others to, and Geoffrey was a concern as he was not getting cleared for migration. It was only after the parents passed away that he was able to migrate on compassionate grounds as the only family member remaining behind. The Surraos are a very well-knit family, something that you don't always see in other large families. It was a do or die effort to reach the Promised Land, come what may. In the case of this family, it was for the better. Four of Cedric's brothers live at Werribee, a new suburb near St. Albans. It was heart-warming to see them stay within handshaking distance of each other, living so comfortably on a street that could easily be called Surrao Street!

Fig 11. Lena and Sylvester Surrao

"What about your dad and mom?" I enquired. "They didn't want to come here," Cedric said. "Mom was unable to do so because of a brush with TB (tuberculosis) and then later in life had Parkinson's disease. Dad wanted to stay with her. After Mom passed away in 1993, Dad migrated to Australia but returned to India in September 1996. His heart always remained in Royapuram and he wanted to be buried alongside Mom." He passed away in Royapuram in October 1996, a month after he returned. It seemed almost as if he had a premonition of his end when he chose to return to his home in Royapuram.

Cedric's mother Lena was a soft-spoken and gentle lady who never seemed to lose her composure although she often looked tired as she struggled with the responsibility of managing a large family. Cedric's father Sylvester was a taciturn gentleman who kept very much to himself though he was a man of many talents. He was an avid photographer and developed black and white photos in a small laboratory in the house and was a voracious reader with a large collection of books. He was kind-hearted, although a man of few words, and gave tuitions in mathematics free of cost to needy children.

The migration of the Anglo-Indians out of India has led to several situations of families being split apart or ageing parents left behind to lead a lonely life. On a harsher vein, some say that the elderly had been abandoned and that money sent from abroad is not enough. Deep down I know that Cedric and his brothers would have regretted not having their parents with them. There can never be a final word in this debate.

Rodney Waples lives in a beautiful house in Camberwell. This is a much more upscale locality than Wantirna, clearly evidenced by the quality of the houses, the tree-lined roads and the lush gardens in front of each of the houses. Rodney retains an aristocratic bearing and maintains a beautifully kept house and garden. He spends his time these days looking after their grandchildren and tending to the garden with a bit of golf thrown in now and again.

Fig 12. Rodney and Gloria

Rodney poured out a drink of whisky for me while he stuck to his preferred red wine. We talked about his early days in Australia. He migrated in 1970, one of the earliest from Royapuram to do so. "I came here with just $7 in my pocket and nothing but hope for the future. Peter Pountney met me at the airport and helped me along in the initial days," he said. "I owe a lot to Peter. He was a really good friend," added Rodney. He sponsored his younger brother Darryl in 1976 and his mother Theresa and father Desmond joined them in 1986 after their retirement from lucrative jobs in banks.

Rodney had a rather puritanical upbringing. He speaks with an air of resignation, "My father and grandfather belonged to the Church of England unlike most of the other Anglo-Indians in Royapuram, who were Roman Catholics. This kept me on the fringe of social activities in Royapuram." The senior Waples' were strict about not allowing Rodney to show interest or even remotely consider marrying a Catholic girl. Their influence on the religious orientation was so strong that Theresa, who was a Catholic, had to convert to the Church of England before she married Rodney's father. It was not just me, after all, who had restrictions of form, formality and stereotyping imposed by well-meaning elders. I would never have thought that Rodney went through the same difficulties as I did as a youngster.

Values and beliefs have changed beyond recognition now. Cedric is a Roman Catholic and Sheryl belongs to the Church of England. She told me that Cedric had insisted that their children be brought up as Catholics. This surprised me as Cedric never displayed any attachment to religion in all the years I knew him. He could only have been following the dictates of the Roman Catholic Church and was bound to the church's rules of inter-marriages. Sheryl didn't object but observed that it didn't matter as Cedric never went to church in any case. The children were left to follow whichever faith they chose to and so it should be. Now in retirement, Cedric goes to the same church as Sheryl; St. John's Anglican Church, which is a short distance from their house. Both of them devote a lot of their time to assisting and offering their services to the church. Cedric also helps keep the books of account for the church. How gracefully the wheel of life spins.

"My paternal grandfather Arthur had a British father and that is the English lineage of the Waples family," Rodney said. A clear and relatively close lineage to a Brit is a source of pride to a blue-blooded Anglo. He lived with the family at 66, West Mada Church Street and doted over the grandchildren though he was always a disciplinarian. Food in the Waples household had a British influence. While lunch was curry and rice, dinner, which was strictly at 7.30 pm, was soup, rolls and salads. "Grandpa Arthur always came to dinner dressed in a suit and tie," he remembered. Rodney's upbringing is reflected a lot in his present lifestyle and even food habits, which continue to this day.

Fig 13. Rodney and Thersa Waples

His mother Theresa, who lives at Nobel Park in a two-room apartment, alone now as her husband Desmond passed away in

2007, is a remarkable lady with a radiance and zest for life rarely seen in an 87-year-old. Her fair countenance and regal bearing make her look like a well-to-do British lady. It was Theresa who wanted the family to migrate all along as she felt this was in their best interest. Rodney, at 21 years, took the plunge into the unknown. Theresa said, "The day he left I was heartbroken." When he left India, there would have been more than a few strings tugging at his heart. In those days communication was largely through letters that took weeks to arrive. There was no FaceTime or Skype or Facebook, and when a 21-year-old left home to take roots in a faraway country, it must have been hugely emotional.

Cedric and I went to St. Albans, where we met Desmond and Geraldine Holt and then Errol and Nigel Edmonds, the twins who were a few years junior to us in St. Mary's and subsequently graduated from the same engineering college as we did. Errol says with a touch of pride, "I am a licensed fundraiser in the state of Victoria, which means all my fundraising activities are audited by the Australian government." He puts in commendable effort every year to raise funds for charitable institutions in India. "It's hard work, man," he says. Nigel, his brother, is a cool customer. He responds to my query, "I am into consulting these days in the elevator industry." He adds with a touch of pride, "I built a career in the elevator industry in India, working first for Best and Crompton and then Kone. I walked into an assignment with Kone in Melbourne."

Fig 14. Nigel, Cedric and Errol

I don't think I ever had anything other than the most casual of friendships with Errol. I was keen on re-establishing contact with him mainly because of his philanthropic activities. Errol and I didn't take long to strike up a warm friendship. He remembered, as he said, the ever-present chuckle in my voice as I spoke and I was enamoured by his spirit of service to those in need. Since that meeting in Melbourne, we have remained in very close touch. I was inspired by the annual walking pilgrimages that he has undertaken for the last eight years from Chennai to Vellankani, a distance of 350 kilometres, and accompanied him on the walk in August 2016. We spent ten days together on the pilgrimage, sometimes sleeping on the pavements and sometimes in the corridors of schools or in the halls of churches. The bonds that develop after such an arduous effort are very special indeed.

Fig 15. Desmond and Gerry Holt

Desmond and Geraldine migrated to Australia much later than the others, in 2003. In the intervening period, they were engaged with fundraising and in helping the underprivileged Anglo-Indians in Royapuram. Desmond is proud of his contributions to the Anglo-Indian community in Royapuram, "I was the President of the Anglo-Indian Association in Royapuram for a while and Geraldine was a teacher at St. Kevin's for over 30 years. Together we have been actively involved with helping the underprivileged Anglo-Indians in a big way. Gerry and I have been witnesses to the changing times in Royapuram." Gerry has a stern air about her, as can be expected of a school teacher, but does display a softer friendlier side as you get to know her. Desmond is tall and athletic with an eye for detail, which seems to have rubbed off on him from Gerry. Both of them continue to have strong emotional bonds with Royapuram and never fail to go there on visits to India. The Holts celebrated their 40th wedding anniversary in Chennai, where they renewed their wedding vows at St. Mary's Cathedral and then had a lovely reception at Doveton Corrie's school in December 2017.

A few days later, I zipped back to the western suburbs at Truganina to be with my nephew Bobby and his wife Gillean for a few days. Gillean's dad and mom, Melroy and Maureen Nash, were also there and I had a wonderful opportunity to get to know them. Maureen has a matronly look but comes across as very considerate of others. Melroy is slimly built, a spin-off from his sporting days in his youth. The Nash brothers were all good hockey players; Eugene played for ITC, Melroy for Ashok Leyland and Charles for TVS. My three-day stay was made all the more pleasant because of the thoughtful consideration shown by Maureen and Melroy to make me comfortable.

Towards the end of 2014, Maureen and Melroy moved into Gillean and Bobby's house. It was on the urging of Bobby and Gillean that they finally agreed to the move. Gillean recollects that her Australian friends were aghast that her parents were going to stay with them indefinitely. She and Bobby, on the other hand, thought it only natural that the ageing parents should join them. Indian values make caring of the parents a God-given duty. The Western world has for long handed over this task to a well-established and flourishing industry that cares for the aged and infirm. Even in India, retirement homes and homes for those who need intensive care are growing in popularity. The choice in our country still remains very much with the elderly. In the Western world, it is expected of the elderly to move to a retirement home.

Maureen was by far the most talkative of the group and told me of the struggle they had to get to Australia. "We migrated to Australia in 1996 after a string of rejected applications, oh God," she said. "We went on an appeal after the third rejection and I really fought hard with them," the resolute lady said. After the hearing and Maureen's spirited defence, they were cleared much to the relief of the parents. Gillean, however, said, "My sister and I cried all the way through the journey to Australia as we were leaving our boyfriends behind." Gillean returned to Chennai in 1999 to get married to Bobby, my brother Ravi's son, and then to work on his immigration visa. Bobby finally migrated in June of 2001.

During my stay, Bobby celebrated his birthday with a rousing party. His friends and musician partners were there and they entertained us with the popular songs of the day and several of their own compositions. Bobby is technically not an Anglo-Indian but his mother's heritage has left a discernible mark on him. He has imbibed the best of both worlds.

Gillean's cousins, Ruth and Jude, are still in India. Ruth, who married Craig Williams, was one of just a few families who lived in Royapuram till they moved to Madhavaram in 2016. It was Ruth who gave me a good understanding of life in Royapuram after the Anglo-Indians left and in the new Anglo-Indian or should I say, Christian settlement of Madhavaram.

Fig 16. Craig and Albert MacDonald

A meeting with Albert and Craig McDonald in the western suburb of Langwarrin was special. The McDonalds were very good friends of my brother Ravi. I remember one day in the sixties the family came down from Pallavaram to Royapuram to spend the day with us, replete with a picnic hamper, straw hats, a cricket bat and a tennis ball. As a young teenager living in a rather straitjacketed way, I was awestricken by their high-spirited and open displays of emotion by both the males and the females in the group. It was a fun-filled day which has always stayed deep down in my storehouse of happy memories. Memories of that one-off visit to our house gave me the strong urge to meet Albert. It was in recognition that the McDonalds fully represented the spirit of the Anglo-Indian zest for living that I secretly yearned for so much. With only vague memories, I still harboured lots of regard for the man and what he represented for me.

Albert worked for some time at a printing press in Royapuram and would commute all the way from Pallavaram to Royapuram, a distance of over 30 kilometres, every day. He would take an electric train to Beach station and then walk the last four kilometres to the printing press or hitch a free ride on the back of a tram. In his late eighties, Albert retains a lively spirit and is remarkably fit and active. He knew little about me other than that I was Ravi's brother; nevertheless, he was full of warmth as we chatted in his drawing room. Sadly, most of his siblings have passed away and so has his wife. His son Craig, now in his fifties, gave up lucrative career options to be at home with his ailing mother. Albert would certainly have moments of grief at the loss of most of his family but never showed this even briefly in the time we spent together. We had lunch at Frankston, a beachside resort near Langwarrin. That day I made a new set of friends in Albert and Craig.

I had climbed the mountain of nostalgia where hermit memories live. Reconnecting with my classmates from good old St. Mary's gave me the resolve to go to the ole' school to soak in the atmosphere of the past never-to-be-forgotten days. It is at school that my association with the Anglos grew but first, let's take a look at Royapuram in the sixties and seventies.

The Heydays of Royapuram

It was a guided tour of the Royapuram I never knew, the dreaded Anglo-Indian quarters. Maureen wistfully says, "Nine out of ten houses on the four Mada Church streets around St Peter's church, Arathoon road and PV Kovil Street were Anglo-Indian homes, man. All the old popular English songs, Jim Reeves, Pat Boone and all would blare out from the Radio Ceylon channel from each home." Marie butted in with a smile, "My, it was the same song from every house." Maureen hadn't finished. "The smell of curries cooking was everywhere," she said with more than a touch of glee. Cedric remembers sauntering off to play in the by-lanes with his pals Bonita Edmonds, Lynette Smith, Everit Mackinon, Ricardo and Lloyd Castellas and a few others. Not to be outdone, Gillean said, "After school, my cousins and I would go to our grandmother's house on PV Kovil Street and play in the little compound of her house and on the street. It was time for rounders, seven- tiles and hide and seek." There was far less traffic on the streets then and Royapuram was one big playground for the young. It was common to find groups of friends gathered at street corners engaging in the social necessity of those days, just chit-chatting.

Young children of both sexes learnt to dance almost mandatorily as this was a prime social activity for Anglo-Indians. Social events such as whist drives, singing competitions and even sporting events where friends and family members gather to cheer on their respective teams all offered platforms for the young to meet and form partnerships. Gillean said, "In the afternoons, after an enforced siesta, our grandmother would get us all together to learn dancing. The elder and better dancers would help the younger ones."

From somewhere in the background we could hear a guitar strumming and voices singing a few bars of a popular song. Singing was a way of life for the Anglo-Indians. Marie said as she interrupted her humming, "My family loved music. My maternal and paternal uncles and my brothers George and Tony played the guitar, violin and piano. I have beautiful memories of my sister Ethel and me singing together from the age of five. My uncle Eugene would accompany us on the guitar or piano. We also sang a few times at the periodic amateur nights conducted at the Parish Hall and later, Ethel also sang with Raymond Potter, whom she married."

Marie added, humming and smiling at the same time, "In the mid-sixties/mid-seventies my two childhood friends, Philo Scurville, May Noronha, and I formed a singing group called 'The Cascades' and we were invited to sing at most Anglo-Indian functions all over Chennai. Even now, when we meet at family get-togethers, we still sing some of our old favourites like *Love of my Life, Sunglasses* and *Rhythm of the Rain*." Bobby promptly got Marie and Ethel to sing *Sun Glasses* as he strummed on the guitar.

There was much of the life of old Royapuram that I had let slip by but I can never forget the Sunday evenings at the Mater Dolorosa Parish club where 16mm movies would be screened on the premises of the church. We got to see some very good movies and enjoyed them very much. The tickets for these shows were four annas to sit on the ground and watch and eight annas to sit on a chair but you had to bring your own chair. "Remember the movies at Mata Dolorosa Church?" I asked the group. "Oh yes," they said in unison. Cedric chipped in, "The projector used to be operated by Rudy Watts, who had strict instructions from the priests to block off kissing scenes with the help of a small cardboard piece that blanked the screen during these "objectionable" scenes." Everyone laughed. "He was popularly called Cardboard Watts," added Marie.

The Mater Dolorosa Parish club was a beehive of activities; something I observed from afar in those days. Whist drives, tombola, dance sessions, amateur music festivals and much more took place at regular intervals. I would have loved to join in but I must admit to being a little apprehensive about entering 'their' land. Desmond Holt chose to be the spokesperson for the group as he said, "MC D'Souza, who was for over a decade the secretary of the club, was instrumental in keeping the club active. Picnics at Mahabalipuram, Kovalam beach and Ennore among other places of interest were popular and well-attended activities." Errol said, "My sister Bonita has tonnes of photos of those days, man." Daphne looked skywards and said, "I think I have a few too." I never got to see any of those photos though. The Anglo-Indians are a fun-loving and hospitable community. They live for the day and enjoy themselves.

One always associated the church as the hub of social activity. Memories linger of our Anglo-Indian friends setting off for church on Sunday mornings dressed, as they say, in their Sunday best. The church would overflow and many people could be seen standing around outside. The choir represented the best of singing talent in the community and their talents spilt over into carol singing in the days leading up to Christmas. "WJ Fernandez was the choirmaster. Everyone went to the midnight Mass because of the beautiful singing," said Marie.

When it came to Christmas time there was a cacophony of voices. Everyone had something to say and there was palpable joy and nostalgia in the group. "It was so much fun as the carol singers went from house to house in a gaily decked and petromax lit open bus singing carols," said Gillean. Marie recollects, "We especially loved the month of December when we would go carol singing, sometimes in a school bus or open top lorry or just walking around the streets of Royapuram with lamps, in the still of the night. Bleary-eyed folks would switch on their house lights to acknowledge our group and hand over envelopes with donations which were used to buy clothes and provide Christmas lunch for the less privileged families."

I never had the opportunity to mingle among the crowd of revellers and carol singers but Christmas carols bring back such fond memories of childhood days and the Christmas spirit that I love to listen to carol singers singing the age-old favourites even today. At home, 'our' place, we always listened to Christmas carols and the love for those old classics has never faded. For me, it is all about the memories that come flooding back as I listen. Yet I never once ventured into the real world, 'their' world, to listen to the guitars strumming and the beautiful voices raised in song. I wish I had the nerve to break free from whatever bonds that chained me down to experience the warmth and love of those occasions.

Years later, in my paying guest days in Bangalore at Frazer Town, groups of kids would come from house to house singing in the most adorable voices and I would listen in rapture. More recently, during a visit to Norman Guido's house in Bangalore, his daughter Lara and her group of carol singers dropped in to sing, all 16 of them. There were young and old and a lady played the piano in Norman's house while others strummed on guitars as the group sang a medley of old Christmas favourites. It was magical.

Maureen Nash talks fondly about Christmas time when dhol dhols, cookies and cakes were made. She said, "The dhol dhols required the entire family to help as it was difficult to stir and cooking on the wood fires also took ages. My mother cooked roast turkey and the thick gravy that was made from the extras. She ran the Bishop Corrie school's canteen for over a decade in the sixties and seventies and definitely knows a thing or two about cooking." Christmas times were when we eagerly awaited plum cakes laced with rum, kulkuls and homemade red wine from our Anglo-Indian friends.

Cedric and Marie said almost together, "The Band Wagon, organised by the Anglo-Indian Association, was the highlight of the Christmas parade with Anglo-Indians and non-Anglo-Indians joining in the festivities." Desmond Holt, with a frown, took over, "Participating families handed over their presents to the organisers to be distributed by 'Santa,' a local or a visiting expatriate, as the parade went around the streets of Mada Church from house to house much to the enthusiasm and excitement of the young and old alike." He added, "A bullock cart was hired and decked up for the occasion along with a marching band from the local police force." Desmond and his wife Gerry were particular about detail and insisted on giving credit where it was due. Gerry said, "In the seventies, this popular event was organised by Laurence Tauro with Henry and Marie Fitzsimmons looking after the logistics of collecting the presents. Later, when Laurence left Royapuram, organisation of the event was taken over by the Fitzsimmons and after them, Desmond and I took over." Desmond chipped in, "The tradition continued when we left for Australia with Garth and Joan D'Cruz taking over the organising of the Christmas functions in Royapuram. When they left, it was Lu Suarez who took over and later Cissy (Doraiswamy) and Jimmy D'Souza assisted by Keith Stephenson and David Antonio. Money was mainly raised by Lloyd D'Souza in Australia from hamper sheets and the Anglo-Indian community organised dances to raise funds for repatriation to Royapuram, with Lorraine Surrao, Gillian Jones and others taking an active part."

My head was in a whirl. All this activity, bullock carts and all, and never once did I get into the milling crowd with 'Santa' bellowing "Ho… ho…" Where was I then? Where else but in the protected little haven of 'our' place far from the din of activity and fun. I wondered if my brothers Gopi and Ravi had ever been among the revellers. "Oh yes," said a voice from afar. It must have been Gopi. He never misses out on the fun. "I've been there also, I say," added my brother Ravi. *Why the heck didn't you take me?* I thought. "You have to make your own rules," said Gopi, who knew a thing or two about living life on his own terms.

Marie recalls, "One year they organised a Christmas pageant. Mada Church Street was blocked at both ends (with police protection) for the entire evening and was transformed into a magical fairyland; a carnival where Santa slid down a rope from one of the rooftops. There were carollers, Christmas music from loudspeakers, food stalls, laughter, singing and dancing. The entire street was illuminated with Christmas lights and decorations, with excited kids running freely all over the place without any fear of being knocked over by motor vehicles. It was open to everyone."

Not to be outdone, the young brigade added immensely to the Xmas gaiety. Sharon Sharman recalls her salad days, where she and her friends Gillian Nash, Diana Nash, Candy Nash, Ruth Williams, Christian Richard, Dominic Desmier, Mario

Desmier, Shayne D'Costa, Rodney D'Costa and Bobby Baskaran used to play guitars and sing in the Mater Dolorosa Choir. They improvised on old hymns and made up new hymns to the beat of pop music ('Beat Masses,' as they were called), which attracted a huge crowd for Sunday Masses. They formed the youth band, 'The Wings of Harmony,' and sang for many Royapuram weddings. They too used to organise pound parties and picnics at Kovalam beach. During the Christmas season, they would go from house to house singing carols; the money collected would be donated to Sishu Bhavan (A home for orphaned children run by Mother Theresa's Sisters of Charity). Sharon wistfully says, "Those were the best fun times we had till most of the crowd either moved to Australia or out of Royapuram."

Theresa Waples, the senior statesperson who shuffled along with the group as we walked along the old haunts of Royapuram, stopped the group by the old railway station and said with a touch of gravity, "The Anglo-Indian colony in Royapuram originated around the railway station like most other Anglo-Indian colonies across the country. The Royapuram railway station was the first to be built by the British in Southern India and was inaugurated in 1856." The Railway Institute club was home to many Anglo-Indian jam sessions and other social events. While still on times gone by in the days of trams, Theresa Waples remembers the merry-go-rounds and food stalls that would come up along South Mada Church Street during Easter. Everyone would go around greeting each other as Theresa says, "If you miss greeting anyone they would tell your mother and you would get a good kicking."

Christmas was a time for giving and the large-hearted Anglo-Indians contributed generously. Gerry Holt predictably stepped in to give credit to all those who deserved it the most. She said, "Arlene DeSouza, Philo Lobo, Joan D'Cruz and I, together with our husbands Llyod, Francis, Garth and Desmond, worked round the clock to get money for the hampers and the Christmas treats for the less fortunate children." The events were spearheaded by this enthusiastic group who arranged for the collection of gifts and provisions from the residents as well as ex-residents and were distributed to needy children and their parents at the grounds of St Kevin's. Anglo-Indians freely donate to those in need even when they themselves can barely make ends meet.

Fig 17. WJ Fernandez on his 100th birthday

No narrative of Royapuram can neglect the role that WJ Fernandez played for decades as he encouraged the less privileged of the community to complete their education and to study beyond high school. WJ was a philanthropist at heart and initiated several measures to raise funds to support the education of needy children. Errol and Cedric were active members of the group that helped WJ in these fundraising activities. Bunny Peters said, "WJ was also the secretary of the St. Mary's Old Boys

Association, which unfortunately split from the official alumni association of the school on what might have been differences of opinion with Rev. Father Whyte and some of the teaching staff of the school."

"Oh, is that why you and Owen used to have such animated conversations on the topic?" added Patti. WJ was, as I said earlier, the Choir Master and took an active part in the activities of the church. His sons Neville and Owen continue this tradition in Australia. WJ's was a life of service to the community and he lived to be 102.

Fig 18. Kunhiraman's Stores

It was inevitable that the group filled with nostalgia would stop by at the Kunhiraman's corner shop, a popular meeting place for all the little groups, hanging around and talking as they ordered mango ice cream or grape juice or fresh lime soda. Kunhiraman's store is an institution that time has left unchanged over the last 50 years or so. It was amazing to see that the shop had not changed one bit. We all ordered grape juice and mango ice cream; both tasted just the same as it did years ago. Bobby ordered tiny samosas which everyone gobbled up. Kunhiraman's store lives on.

Persian Bakery was another institution of the day. Errol fondly remembered, "Gajapathy, who spoke English with the distinctive Anglo-Indian slang with bits of Tamil thrown in, was the popular owner. Persian Bakery made excellent wedding cakes that were popular all across Chennai among the community." Royapuram was blessed with two excellent bakeries, the second being Royapuram Bakery on East Mada Church Street. Errol adds, "Royapuram Bakery was run by Moorthy and their wedding cakes too were the talk of the town, with people coming from as far away as Arakonam, man, to buy cakes." Royapuram Bakery also offered the additional service of baking homemade cakes and also roasting turkeys during Christmas times. Maureen goes gaga when she remembers Royapuram Bakery and says, "I loved their horseshoe and chocolate cakes and the unforgettable mouth-watering buns." We meandered towards Ideal Stores where we would once go to pick up gifts and knick-knacks from time to time. Who can forget the barber shop on West Mada Church Street? That nondescript place where all of us went for our haircuts; nothing fancy like the salons of today.

Anglo-Indians love their hockey, football and cricket. Desmond conducted the group to St Peter's compound where spectators once used to sit on the compound wall and friends and family used to gather at the grounds to cheer for their teams. "Matches were arranged between various groups; bachelors versus married men, Anglo-Indians versus non-Anglo-Indians, Catholics versus Protestants and between cricket clubs," said Cedric. He added, "Desmond Holt, Gerry and Andy Duarte and I were most active in arranging these matches and tournaments." It was picnic time as much as it was cricketing time. Desmond, a pace bowler and batsman who came very close to representing the state cricket team, and Cedric formed a team called the Royapuram Colts built around the Anglo-Indians of Royapuram. The team just missed qualifying for the 5th Division League in Chennai before taking over another club that was in the 4th Division League.

Desmond added a bit about association life in Royapuram while most of the others seemed lost in thought. "Gerry and I were very active members of the Anglo-Indian community in Royapuram. I served as the Secretary of the Association when Neville Fernandez was the president and took over as the president when Neville moved on to Australia." He went on to say, "The founding president was Mervyn Duarte, in whose name inter-branch cricket and boxing tournaments were conducted along with the associations of Veprey, Perambur, St Thomas Mount, Pallavarum and Santhome for the MSA Duarte Rolling Shield." Gerry said with obvious emotion, "Those were great days in our lives; firmly etched in, never to be forgotten."

When the Association was closed (or derecognised) by the All India Anglo-Indian Association for reasons that were not very clear, four families: the D'Cruzs, the DeSouzas, the Lobos and the Holts continued to engage in fundraising for the less fortunate community members, particularly during Christmas time. Food hampers were arranged for the poor with Desmond and Geraldine working round the clock to prepare and distribute the hampers. Desmond remembers, "Our house was like a Kotwal market with all the foodstuff strewn all over our hall on the eve of Christmas, as we were packing and distributing the hampers to our folks. Only when this was done did we have time to clean and decorate our house for Christmas. Gerry and I believed that it was in giving at Christmas time that was our greatest reward. God has blessed us in so many ways."

We heard the tinkling of a cycle bell and a voice said, "Let's go to the beach." I am sure it was Gopi. For years the Royapuram beach was an iconic landmark of Royapuram. The cool evening breeze from the Bay of Bengal attracted large crowds to the beach in the evenings, eating *sundal* and other snacks offered by street side vendors. Cycling to the beach every evening was an almost mandatory social event. The beach and the rocky shores also offered a treat of crabs on full moon nights and generally in the monsoon months. My dad often bought crabs off the beach from the fishermen and we enjoyed the messy eating that it involved on lazy Sundays. "Sorry Gopi," I was forced to say. The construction of an iron ore port and the extension of the

Royapuram harbour completely consumed the beach beside bringing in iron ore contamination. There is no beach today.

Royapuram was not all about the Anglo-Indians. This little hamlet was an oasis of peace with Parsis, Christians, Muslims, Jains and Hindus living together in harmony. Royapuram boasted of a Parsi Fire temple and a very active Parsi club that held tombola sessions, cards and even cricket matches with the booming voice of Dr. Cooper anchoring most of the events. Theresa Waples reminiscences, "In the days of the British, Royapuram was one of the better suburbs to live in; Judges, Residential Medical Officers of Royapuram Hospital and prominent people such as Mary Clubwalah Jadhav lived on Main Road, which had huge houses with lovely gardens."

It was in 1972, just when the early migrants were leaving for Australia, that I got a job at the Indian Telephone Industries in Bangalore. I was to leave Royapuram to return only from time to time for short vacations. I was now thrown into another world altogether; a world that consumed me totally in mind, body and spirit. I was left with little time for Royapuram and my Anglo-Indian friends. Fittingly, it was an Anglo-Indian, Oscar D'Silva, whom I got to know when I was working as a stipendiary trainee at Philips India, who saw me off. He ran alongside the train waving goodbye to me as the train steamed out of Central Station on its way to Bangalore. As I was leaving home to start a life of my own, my relief knew no bounds. There was no hint of apprehension or anxiety. I was thirsting for the fresh air of freedom.

The face of Royapuram would change dramatically over the years as the Anglo-Indians migrated out, as did the more affluent of the other communities, with industrialisation bringing about increased lorry traffic and pollution besides the hazardous iron ore pollution that hung over the town. Royapuram was inexorably morphing into Lorrypuram.

Our School and Home

Indescribable emotions flickered through me on a visit to our school, St. Mary's, in July 2016. It was almost 50 years since my last visit and I was a trifle unsure of the response I would get. As it turned out the watchman at the gate, a portly but genial individual, gave me a beaming smile when I told him I was an ex-student and led me to the Principal Father Sundar's room. A winning smile from a watchman can be such an icebreaker.

Father Sundar was polite at first but showed more than a touch of warmth as we spoke. He called out to an attendant, "Ask the assistant headmaster to come." Eugene Reddy, a tall and amiable teacher who had none of the stern countenances that we normally associate with headmasters or assistant headmasters, walked into the room with a quizzical look on his face. Father Sundar said pointing to me, "This is an ex-student. He is willing to help us connect with old students whom he knows well." We discussed, among other things, the need for the alumni stepping up to assist the school which manages only off the school fees it collects and receives limited support from the government. I promised to reach out to ex-St. Mary's students I was in touch with to help in whatever way we could.

Eugene asked a couple of bright young students to give me a tour of the school premises. The classrooms had been shuffled around since our days; the earlier standards 5A and 5B now house the senior classes though the classrooms look much the same as they did decades ago. Most of the classrooms were jam-packed with students whether in the primary classes or the senior classes. As I walked around I barged into some of the classes to greet the students and to take photos. Eugene Reddy got me to speak to the students of a class he was teaching just then.

Fig 19. A class room in St. Mary's today

I was struck by the politeness and a refreshing simplicity and exuberance that I saw everywhere I went. The students greeted me cheerfully and some little boys who were sitting outside in the corridors (God forbid they had spilt over) proudly showed me their class books. Father Sundar had told me with a touch of pride, "The medium of education continues to be English.

The school takes care to recruit teachers who are proficient in English."

The classrooms of the original school block looked just the same as in our days in school back in the sixties. The classrooms on the first floor even had the same wooden partitions we had in our days. The library had moved from the little room, manned by Bernard Matthews, on the ground floor to a spacious hall on the third floor. The chemistry, physics and biology labs were also spacious though sparse and could do with additional facilities.

Fig 20. The quadrangle at St. Mary's

I walked up to a window on the first floor that overlooked the quadrangle and pressed my head against the railings just as I had done decades ago on a wet and rainy day. Way back then I had heard a rustling sound behind me and wiped around to see the large figure of Father Whyte standing just behind me. "You look sad," he had said and I had responded, "The weather makes me gloomy, Father."

Father Whyte was a principal we loved and feared at the same time. A voice from nowhere asked, "Is that you, Baskaran?" I whispered back, "Yes, Father. I didn't expect to meet you here." The grave voice continued, "I walk these corridors over and over again these days. Never seem to be able to get out of the place. The stone corridors and stairways have been mute spectators for over 100 years of schooling." "You made the school great, Father," I ventured to say, a lot bolder than I ever could in the past.

"The school is among the oldest in India and one of the first five to be set up by the British in 1839. It was known for over 40 years as St. Mary's Seminary and Day School," he said. "When we joined the school in 1957, it was called St. Mary's European High School and later it was changed to St. Mary's Anglo-Indian High School," I said hesitantly. He gave me a searching look before going on, "The first Principal was Rev. Dr. William Kelly of Maynooth. In 1916 new buildings were constructed and the science laboratory was remodelled and very well equipped. It was considered one of the best science laboratories for high schools at that time. Progress in studies and sports grew rapidly and St Mary's was one of the leading European boys' schools in the Madras Presidency." He had a faraway look in his eyes.

"When did you join as the principal, Father?" I asked, breaking the silence. "I was the principal from 1945 to 1971. Those were the golden years of the school, weren't they?" he asked with a twinkle in his eye. "I celebrated a silver jubilee double," he said with a hearty laugh. "It was all of 25 years in the service of the school and 25 years in the service of the Lord," he went on to say. Suddenly there was an eerie silence and I sensed Father was no longer with me.

Those were the golden days of the school without a shadow of a doubt. He was known to have helped to a great extent the less fortunate of the Anglo-Indian community as Peter Kelly remarked, "Father Whyte used to help the needy Anglo-Indians with books and uniforms, often spending from his own pocket." Besides his great humanism and penchant for humour, he was a great administrator and a boxer in his younger days and strongly believed that boxing as a sport was a great character builder. The school boxing completion used to be held on St. Patrick's Day, also Father Whyte's birthday.

Fig 21. At a meeting of classmates in Melbourne

My meeting with a group of classmates from school at Melbourne in March 2015 was a time for nostalgia and recollection of the good old school days. We associate St. Mary's very much with Rev. Father Whyte and the teachers: Bernard Matthews, Arthur Edmonds, Coelho, Emanuel, Mashallah, Lewis, D'Cruz (Duck Roast), SP Shillong and others. In their own way, each one helped shape us. Many remembered the caning they received from Ft. Whyte. Corporal punishment was not taboo those days and not considered shameful. Daryl Christian recalled with a touch of pride that he too had been caned by Father Whyte. "Father asked me to select a cane," he said. "I picked a thin one but Father changed it to a thicker and more formidable looking one," he added. Rodney remembered how Bernard Mathews had a unique way of pulling you up by your sideburns. Those unfortunate enough to be so punished rose up on their toes as Mathews gradually increased the pull. Sri remembered Lewis getting hapless students to bend over and giving them a few thumps on their backs. Etched in my memory is Coelho sauntering into class with his pyjamas showing out from below his trousers (easy for him to rip off his trousers and relax when at home). Coelho had a brilliant mind and insisted on us learning the tables all the way till 20×20 and wanted us to be comfortable with numbers. He hardly ever taught mathematics and trigonometry as he believed you needed to learn it yourself but prepared a little notebook, a sort of 'tutorial' that the less mathematically inclined could use to pass with credit in the board exams.

The voices from days gone by floated into our memories. Rodney remembered Emanuel talking of 'the 'ellow sands of the Gobi Desert' as he did his best to add interest to geography lessons. Cedric remembered Edmonds saying, "You Surraos have vowed never to pass in the Hindi exams." Arthur Edmond's booming voice and his reading of Julius Caesar, our Shakespeare text in high school, are unforgettable. His rendition of Mark Antony's oration at Caesar's funeral gave me goose pimples in those days. Mathew's was in charge of the library and he was most often in the little library immersed in reading. We would get our quota of Billy Bunter, William, Enid Blyton and other books from the library with Mathews happy to cultivate the reading habit in us. Rodney had an urge to get hold of a Wren and Martin Grammar book, not a recent edition but the little red book we used in our school days. I was later able to get him a vintage 1968 edition from the Blossom's Bookshop on Church Street in Bangalore.

School days were the time for steady development through adolescence to young men. There wasn't any conscious effort that I can remember in this regard. Behaviour, culture and ethos were gradually and subtly ingrained in us. I am sure the impact that the Anglo-Indians had on me in those formative days was immense but it was not a time for excessive self-reflection, so I don't really know what stuck and what didn't. The enduring relationship with Anglo-Indians can only be on account of my seven years in St. Mary's. The influences I was subjected to at home were equally strong. I owe much to my parents, brothers, relatives and the extended family members for what I grew up to be. I felt, at times, trapped between two worlds and didn't have the wherewithal to work my way out of some of the contradictions I saw around me. I was to face up to sterner tests that helped shape me up as a man many years later.

The school now has approximately 1770 students crammed into a rather small floor space. St. Mary's unfortunately never had a playground, so essential to a school. In our days the nearby law college grounds served as a venue for cricket, hockey and athletics practice. Athletics was early in the morning and we were treated to a masala dosa and coffee by the school at the nearby Ramakrishna Lunch Home. It was in our early school days that the Anglo-Indian schools inter-schools meet was resumed and we always did very well in those meets. I understand these grounds are no longer available due to additional construction. To cross the road and get to whatever playfields are left would also be a daunting task given the high level of traffic and construction work going on.

A classmate of yesteryear, Norman Guido, and I met after 50 years in January 2016. Norman went on to become a well-known plastic surgeon and head of the department of plastic surgery at St. John's Medical College and Hospital. We talked at length about our school days, as classmates are wont to, as we sipped our respective drinks. "Sad, we didn't have good playfields," he said. "Yeah," I replied. "We just had a small concrete compound but that did not stop the boys from playing hand cricket, hand tennis, rounders and just flinging tennis balls or even sweet lime peels at each other across two bases of the cemented compound, isn't it?" I added. "I remember our games periods being held at the nearby law college grounds," Norman said. "You remember the regular 'scraps' in the evenings where the contestants went to fight it out, accompanied by their friends," he added. Word would go around that a scrap was on that evening and those interested went to watch. "I understand there are very few Anglo-Indians at St. Mary's these days," Norman remarked. "Yes, Father Sundar told me that in the school strength of 1770 there are just 30 or 40 Anglo-Indians," I said.

St. Mary's believed in holistic education. '*Mens Sana in Corpore Sano*' or a healthy mind in a healthy body was drilled into us. Sports and games were emphasised as much as learning the three Rs (reading, 'riting and 'rithmatic). To be a good human being and to be true to oneself was part of our upbringing. When we meet a St. Maryian, we invariable conclude that he is a good bloke. Father Gregory, the ex-Principal of the school, told me, "The student profile has changed over the years and while most children in the past came from educated households, the students of today largely come from the homes of small businessmen who are generally illiterate." He also readily admits, "The ethos of taking charge of students and building their character is a thing of the past all across the schooling system in the country."

The year 2014 saw a string of activities as the school celebrated its 175th year; besides sports and cultural events, 175 saplings were planted and gifts as well as articles were distributed to 175 underprivileged children and a special First Day Cover was released. The pinnacle of the celebrations was the presence of Dr. APJ Kalam, the much-loved former President of India and a great advocate of quality education, at the 175th Annual Day and Parents Day. Several distinguished alumni were invited to be the chief guests at functions conducted through the year. My dear friend Dr. Mohan Viswanathan, a Padma Shri recipient, was the chief guest of Captain's Day and the release of the First Day Cover.

I was so glad to see that in several places in the Jubilee Souvenir there was mention of Rev. Father Whyte and his immense contribution to the growth and development of the school. In his message, Father Jayapalan Raphael, Provincial, Salesian Province of Chennai said, "Perhaps pride of place goes to Father George Whyte, the long-time principal who made a significant contribution in making St. Mary's what it is today. His 27 years' service to the school can only be described as a saga of devotion and dedication to the cause of the young and especially the poor."

It is sad that many of us old-timers of the school had no part to play in this great year of celebration. I know that Rodney had planned to lead a group of our classmates to participate but many felt there was no point in attending as we had completely lost touch with the school; an unfortunate reflection on the alumni association of the school in this age of social media and digital networking. In stark contrast, the St. George's Homes, Ketti, has an alumni association that is most active. The managing committee of the centenary celebration that was held in 2014 had several members of the alumni with Sailendra Bhaskar, a past student, being the chairman of the committee.

Fig 22. Rev. Father Gregory

Ever since I heard that Father Gregory, the then principal, was the motivating force behind the highly successful 175th-year-anniversary celebration of the school, I was extremely keen to meet him and seek from him his views on how St. Mary's as a school had developed over the years. Father Gregory is a highly considerate priest. He took great pains to see that I did not have difficulty finding his school, Don Bosco Matriculation, Red Hills, Chennai, which he took over as the principal after retiring at the age of 58 from St. Mary's. My conversations with Father Gregory over a few months impressed me greatly. He struck me as a dynamic priestly go-getter who answers phone calls even after ten pm and has 'jovialgregory' as his email id. He gave me a great deal of time on a truly busy day for him and I remain grateful for his consideration and courtesy.

Father Gregory is down to earth and a person who is passionate about his calling and his engagement with projects that benefit the disadvantaged sections of society. "The most meaningful years of my life were the three-year association with the Anbu Illam Project which assists abandoned street children," he said. He continues to be involved with work related to this project and clearly, his heart lies in such endeavours.

Father Gregory proudly says, "I changed the image of St. Mary's in recent times as the school where a student stabbed a teacher to the school that APJ Abdul Kalam visited." He is justifiably proud of the work he did for the 175th centenary celebration of the school. This was a high point in his brief tenure as the principal of St. Mary's; he encouraged the alumni to donate liberally to assist the school in many improvement projects. He is candid about the school's progress over time and believes that the insistence of the state government to follow the prescribed syllabus and textbooks has led to a decline in standards of education. Following such a mandate is necessary because the school is partially assisted financially by the state government. Schools that are privately funded have greater freedom in this regard and have higher standards of education. Nevertheless, in his opinion, St. Mary's remains one of the top-ranking schools among the 48 Anglo-Indian schools in Chennai.

I came away from the meeting very appreciative of a man of action. In every endeavour, he is sure to leave his imprint. May his tribe increase; our schools require such dedicated services.

The school building, the quadrangle and the physical features of the school and its surroundings have remained the same but the student and teacher profiles have changed and the Anglo-Indian presence in the school has gone. The school as we knew it doesn't exist any longer and can only remain in the archives of fond memories.

From Royapuram to Lorrypuram

I soaked in the familiar landmarks as I drove down North Beach Road in Chennai on my way to meet the last of the Anglo-Indian families in Royapuram. They remained amidst the ruins of the Royapuram of old, refusing to migrate or leave. My heart sunk when I saw the iconic SBI building in ruins and falling apart. *How could this ever happen?* I thought. Our house in the early fifties, with its large compound and jamoon trees, towards the end of the Kalmandapam Road, had been demolished and replaced by awful looking flats. I never expected to see the old house; I just wanted to stop there awhile. The emotions of one's early days are difficult to fathom. The old gives way to the new but ever so often the new has so little charm.

Hartland, the home where I grew up, on West Mada Church Street, had also been demolished after we had sold it to a builder in the late eighties. I stopped the car and got down for a while. I could see in my mind's eye the cemented courtyard where we used to play tennis ball cricket and the ring of Ashoka trees that I loved to clamber upon and read or study in solitude. I walked down West Mada Church Street keen to see the institutions that were an integral part of my youth; the Parsi Club, the Mata Dolorosa

Church, St. Kevin's school and the convent where the nuns used to live, the Parsi Fire temple and the Sisters of Charity Home further down the street. My mind was abuzz with fond memories of the past. But this was a bygone era now, to remain only as memories and not to be recreated. The times have changed and our lives have moved on, creating newer memories of battles won and lost and of a life well spent. The days of my youth, with its fond memories, was drowned by more recent memories of the challenges, battles and victories of the succeeding periods of my life.

This poem by Sarojini Naidu says it all:

The new hath come and now the old retires;
And so the past becomes a mountain-cell,
Where lone, apart, old hermit memories dwell
In consecrated calm, forgotten yet
Of the keen heart that hastens to forget
Old longings in fulfilling new desires.

Fig 23. Daphne and family outside their home

The Anglo-Indians had long gone from Royapuram and so had the Parsis as well as most of the families we grew up with. I drove into Mariadas Street where Daphne Sharman, a classmate from class 1 to 4, and her family live. They are one of just a few Anglo-Indian families left in Royapuram. Daphne had demolished their 125-year-old house in 2011 and built a three-storied house in its place. The memories of the old house with its front verandah and tall pillars are now only captured in the old photographs she has retained along with some exquisite memorabilia. She brought out from the storeroom an ancient 1896 newspaper, aged and crumbling; it would have fallen apart if you ventured to turn the pages. The treasures of over 100 years were packed in a little cardboard box, forgotten and unattended, just like the memories that reside crammed in a corner of our brain. I just had to reproduce this beautifully maintained marriage proposal dated 1926 along with a formal letter of acceptance. Many Anglo-Indian families would have similar letters of a beautiful Anglo-Indian tradition tucked away in a treasure chest.

Blusavel.
20th. August. 1926

Dear Mrs Dique,

You are probably already aware that I have ventured to make a proposal of marriage to your Daughter Cissy, and I am proud and happy to say that subject to your approval, she has accepted my addresses. I now write to ask for your consent to our engagement, and to our marriage, when you shall deem fit, for I am in no hurry, and would wait.

to say that I am in I am thankful excellent health

2

and in a suitable position as a Driver,
and can assure you that I can
satisfy you; as to my character and
social fitness, as to aspire to your
daughter's hand. I shall be happy
to satisfy you on any point upon
which you desire further information,
if you will kindly grant me an
interview for that purpose.

I wish you will make
us happy by giving your consent to
my engagement, with your Charming
daughter, to whom I am entirely and
sincerely devoted, and for whose
happiness I shall ever strive

I have admired Cissy
for months, and she has reciprocated
my love. And so I trust that this

3

deep and true affection may plead with you who have always shown me much kindness.

Hoping and waiting anxiously for a favourable reply with kindest regards.

I remain

Your Sincerely and Respectfully

Edward. Browne.

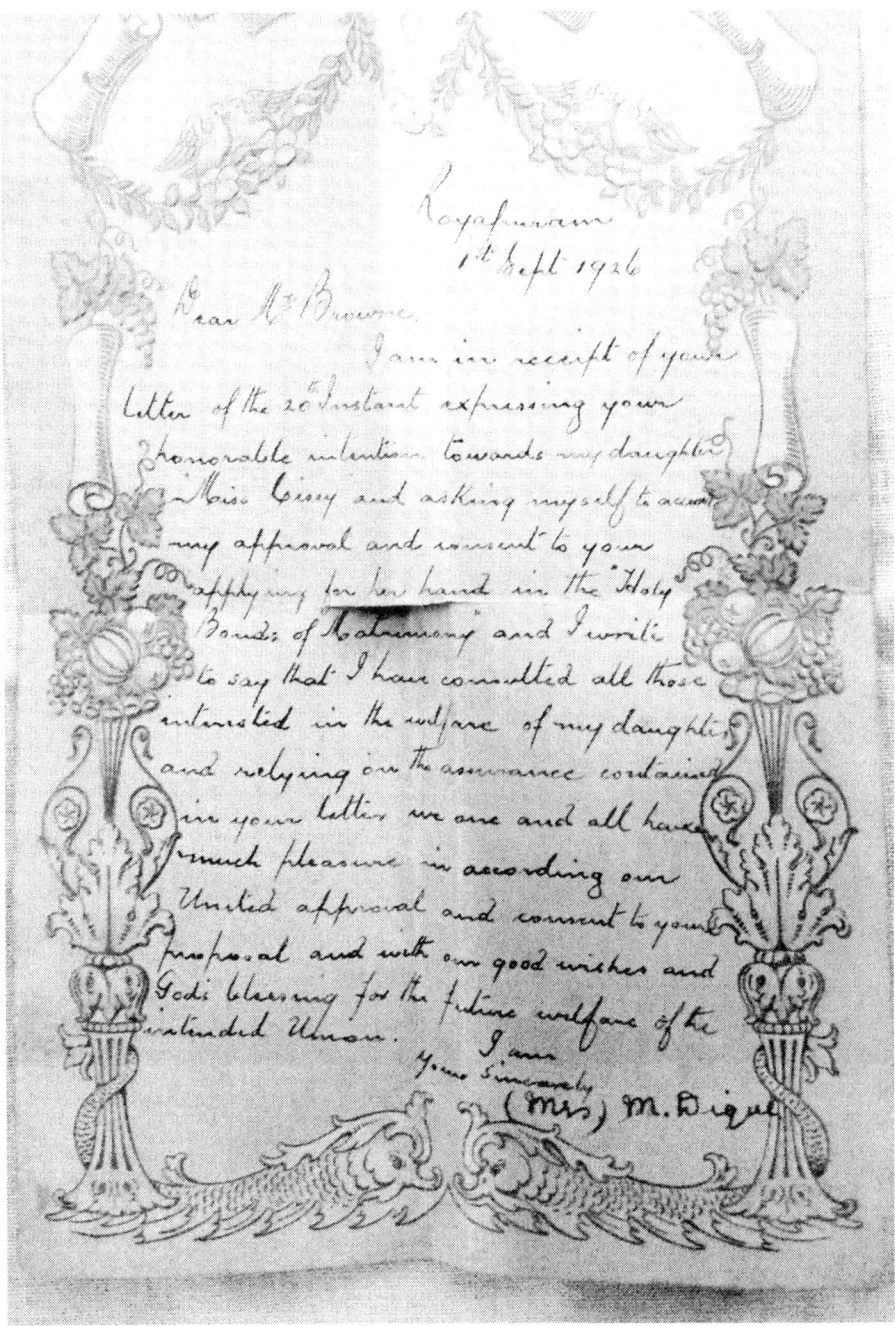

Rayapuram
1st Sept 1926

Dear Mr Browne,

I am in receipt of your letter of the 20th Instant expressing your honorable intention towards my daughter Miss Cissy and asking myself to accord my approval and consent to your applying for her hand in the "Holy Bonds of Matrimony" and I write to say that I have consulted all those interested in the welfare of my daughter and relying on the assurance contained in your letter we one and all have much pleasure in according our United approval and consent to your proposal and with our good wishes and God's blessing for the future welfare of the intended Union.

I am
Yours Sincerely
(Mrs) M. Dique

I spent several hours of fun and laughter with Daphne, her daughter Sharon, son-in-law Binu and son Clinton. It was a time to rapidly catch up with all that happened in our lives over half a century and the naughtiness of early school days. Daphne recollected, amidst peals of laughter, how she surreptitiously rang the school bell hours ahead of scheduled closing time, resulting in scores of children running off home and overturning a startled nun whose headgear fell off revealing a smooth bald pate.

Fig 24. Daphne, Binu, Sharon and Clinton

The buzz of conversation and jokes went on as we sat around the lunch table. Daphne and Sharon had cooked a sumptuous meal of coconut milk rice, chicken vindaloo, Andhra chicken, meat and potato cutlets and an onion and ginger paste chutney. To cool our palates, we had grape juice and the desert was mango ice cream, both Kunhiraman's favourites. It was a thoughtful touch by Daphne.

Fig 25. St. Kevin's from Daphne's archives of photos

We talked about the Anglo-Indian families migrating to Australia and other countries. With the faintest of resignations in her voice, Daphne said, "When you have family responsibilities and have to take care of elderly family members, you never think of going away and leaving them alone to fend for themselves in a home for the aged." With conviction, she adds that the financial health of the family was strong and they had the ability to lead a comfortable life in India. The family's decision may have hung in the balance for a while, but with the situation having changed for the better in India and job opportunities as well as the potential to earn a decent wage being quite good, the family voted to stay. I say it was a family vote as the children too were clear that they would not choose to migrate to a country where they would be treated as second-class citizens. Sharon, in particular, lost a lot of her friends to the wave of migration. It was then or never as the family chose to remain in the country.

Sharon works in the World Bank in the HR department and has graduated with a bachelor's degree in literature from Stella Maris College. Clinton graduated from the Government College of Fine Arts and has also equipped himself with a course in graphics design. He currently works for a graphics design firm. Sharon has never experienced negative stereotyping as an Anglo-Indian. Clinton too is very comfortable with his friends circle and is bemused when asked if he misses the company of Anglo-Indian friends. Daphne claims to be a bit of a recluse not given to an active social life and does not miss the Anglo-Indian dance and jam sessions. She says tongue in cheek, "If all the Anglo-Indians go away then to whom can the visiting Anglo-Indians boast about the glorious land of opportunity they have migrated to." In keeping with the changing times, Sharon has married a Malayali from Cochin. For good measure, Daphne quotes a well-known Sir Walter Scott poem:

Breathes there the man, with soul so dead,

Who never to himself had said,

This my own, my native land!

Daphne and her family are unperturbed by the changes in demographics or the pollution. This was their native land.

Ruth Williams says, "Anglo-Indians in India today are willing to compete with everyone else for jobs. Reservations are a thing of the past. We are no longer laid back and now study beyond high school and make the most of the opportunities. We too now aspire to own houses and make a mark in society." This sentiment is echoed by many Anglo-Indians I spoke to. They see increasing evidence of Anglo-Indians competing successfully and doing well in various fields.

Ruth had this to say of the time when almost every house in Royapuram was an Anglo-Indian home. "There were family members living a few houses away and across the street. It was natural for the community to remain cloistered and cling to their way of living. Now there are just a few Anglo-Indian families in the whole of Royapuram. My young children are growing up in the midst of other communities and seek to dress and speak like them. We are not worried that they will lose their Anglo-Indian identity and be seen as Tamils. Changes have taken place all around us. Services in the church are conducted in Tamil. The children in school tend to speak in Tamil and learning Tamil is mandatory in schools." Ruth adds, "The Christmas celebrations and carol singing are no longer what they were in the sixties and seventies. The popular TV serials are now in Tamil or Hindi and the children and the elders, for that matter, have got used to watching them."

When Royapuram was an Anglo-Indian town, other community members needed to accept the Anglo way of life to be able to fit in.

Today Royapuram is no longer an Anglo-Indian town and residents follow their own customs and practices. All of them tend to celebrate festivals across community lines. Ruth says, "In the old days in Royapuram you could identify a Christian house when a star was lit up outside the house and there was a Christmas tree inside. Now even non-Christian houses do the same. Diwali is celebrated at most houses, irrespective of communities, and homes are lit up and crackers burst." And so it should be in any town. All communities need to co-exist and participate in each other's festivals.

Ruth is not ready to drop everything and migrate to Australia because everyone else has. She has adjusted well and does not see the need to do so except on economic considerations just as it is for people across communities in India today. Her brother Jude has married a Hindu, reflecting the trend in India of marriages across communities. The boundary lines across caste, religion and language have definitely blurred.

In August 2016, Ruth and family finally moved from Royapuram to Madhavaram. Attachments to places grow on you and in spite of the pollution, congestion and the menace of lorries, Ruth refused to shift although her brother and husband kept insisting that they should. She felt that Madhavaram was back of beyond and she didn't want to go to such an isolated place. When finally she did agree to move, she found it heavenly. As Ruth says, "Madhavaram is far less polluted and we have the luxury of an independent place to stay with more play area and space for the kids and us to stretch around. There are many more Anglo-Indian families here. The New Year's dance at St. Sebastian's church hall was strictly for Anglo-Indians only. It was lovely to be part of something like that after ages."

Madhavaram is the new Royapuram. Way back in the eighties and nineties, Anglo-Indians from Royapuram and other parts of Chennai found Madhavaram an ideal location to settle in as land values were still reasonable and many could afford to invest in houses. Rents and the cost of living had been increasing in other parts of Chennai and owning a house was a sensible option. Many Anglo-Indians who bought houses in Madhavaram have since migrated to Australia; while some have sold their houses, others have retained them and given them out on rent or leased it out for fixed periods of time.

Over 30 Anglo-Indian families still live in Madhavaram and the morning and evening services at the church have a high presence of the community. The broader Christian community, which includes Tamilian Christians besides the Anglo-Indians, meets every month at each other's house by rotation in each area. Bible study sessions are conducted separately in Tamil and English with the English sessions conducted by members of the Anglo-Indian community. At Christmas time each area is abuzz with activities and carol singing. Ruth's joy knew no bounds when after years she witnessed a bandwagon going around the streets of Madhavaram distributing gifts to the children. Ruth exclaimed, "It revived beautiful memories of the good old days in Royapuram. I took pictures and sent it to my friends in Australia."

The character of Royapuram has changed like so many other towns in India. It is not just an Anglo-Indian phenomenon. The very fabric of society has changed and most of the time is spent at work or in leisure with the family. Close-knit friends' circles of the past have given way to transitory groups. Loyalty to places and friendships are less prevalent these days.

Conclaves of Anglo-Indians all over the country were equally witness to this sad migration of a vibrant and fun-loving community. The same is true of neighbouring Pakistan. In an article dated 2011, Masood Hasan writes nostalgically of a lost era, "At the hangouts, Karachi particularly and Lahore catching up all the time, and Sam's in Murree, the Anglo-Indians could set a floor on fire as they jived, jitterbugged, rocked & rolled, swung, waltzed or shook sensuously to Latin-flavoured mind-blowing melodies. And it was on the dance floors that you saw girls who could break your heart with just a look, hair tossing, laughing their pretty heads off as adept and handsome male escorts took them through the paces." He moans the migration of the community as he writes, "Those of us who grew up with them watched with considerable sadness as family after family left this country to go and live in alien climes… They left by the droves, never to come back. The clubs died, the dance floors uprooted, the many services they offered fell by the wayside." And so, it was all over the sub-continent.

A new lifestyle has engulfed the young and old of our country. The pace of life has increased and community entertainment has given way to cosmopolitan pastimes. Song and dance and club life once so dear to the Anglo-Indians is a passion across communities. There is little need to moan the loss of the lifestyle of yesteryear but there is definitely a need to preserve the heritage of the past and it is sad that in Royapuram there is no heritage site that keeps alive the memory of the Anglo-Indians. It is heart-wrenching to see the degradation in the quality of life, the loss of the higher values of good living to material craving and the disregard as well as irreverence for the heritage of the past.

The extension of the harbour and the creation of an iron ore handling port are examples of the deterioration of the quality of life. It impacted the demographics of Royapuram almost as much as the migration of the Anglo-Indians. This development completely wiped out the beach. The ideal setting for social confluence had been consumed by the march of industrialisation. The iron ore loading and unloading created a major crisis of iron ore pollution. This led the upper middle class and the affluent to move to other parts of Chennai or the rest of the country. In their wake came the traders and the real estate agents with their penchant for demolishing old houses and building multiple dwelling units where once stood proud bungalows.

A report in the Hindu newspaper, dated 12th June 2003, titled *Pollution Perils in Royapuram* says, "In Royapuram, during summer a tinted inshore wind turns everything into a shade of red. From leaves to clothes and from your pet dog to the frothing milk, the colour of the season is red. The reason for this is visible from the roof of the MV Hospital-mountains of iron ore (it is dark red coloured soil) that silhouette the sky." The report goes on to say, "In January, 10,000 residents including 5000 children from local schools formed a human chain to highlight the effects of the breath-defying breeze."

After a high court order banning the handling of dusty pollutants such as iron ore and coal by the Port Trust at the Royapuram harbour, the iron ore handling facilities were shifted to the Kamarajar Port at Ennore in 2011. Pollution levels at Royapuram are lower now but nowhere near the desired levels.

With the modernisation of the port facilities, many labourers lost their jobs leading to a search for alternate sources of livelihood. They moved to trades relating to logistics and the food grain polishing industries that came up along the major roads. The expanded industrial activity around the harbour and the growth of the industrial belt north of Royapuram led to a steep increase in lorry traffic. The din of speeding lorries with blaring horns ran through the night. During the day it was common to see row on row of lorries parked at vantage points; the compound wall of St. Peter's church is one such point. Cedric told me that on a visit to Royapuram some years ago he saw a line of lorries parked along the road in front of what used to be his home. It hurt him so much he didn't want to go back there again.

Royapuram has inexorably become Lorrypuram.

Dawn of a New Era

Rodney was dressed in a suit as he set off in February 1970 for Melbourne by a circuitous route that took him via Colombo, Kuala Lumpur, Sydney and Melbourne with just $7 in his pocket. This was his maiden flight and it could not have been more path-breaking. Rodney experienced a sense of awe and excitement besides the numbing feeling of flying out into the unknown. He didn't know what was in store for him but at the age of 21, positive anticipation outweighed the apprehension in his thoughts.

Dressing up for the occasion reflects the importance placed on an event or activity. For Rodney, this was the greatest moment of his life in those heady days of yesteryear and a suit seemed appropriate for the occasion. "I perspired a lot during the breaks in the journey," he said. On a similar journey now, he would set off in a pair of jeans, a semi-formal shirt and a pair of trendy casual shoes. Rodney has come a long way since that fidgety nervous flight in 1970. He and his wife Gloria have travelled extensively around the globe to some of the most sought-after holiday destinations in the world.

Blossom recollects with a smile, "I dressed up in my very best outfit and a pair of high-heeled shoes and makeup suitable for a party as I set off to attend my first interview in Melbourne. I thought it was going to be a secretarial job but it turned out to be a back office assignment in the basement of the firm," she said. She was selected for the post and her interviewer told her that she didn't need to be so dressed up when she came to work! She must have been flabbergasted to see Blossom dressed in party wear. Getting a job, any job, as quickly as possible is a migrant's foremost desire. Who will blame them for dressing up for the occasion?

Fig 26. Blossom and Srivatsa

Rodney remembers, "I used to pour over the classified advertisements in the newspapers searching for appropriate jobs. I didn't know the geography of the city and often picked assignments too far away from where I was staying." Response to job vacancies called for making a phone call which he found quite daunting initially. He found it tough to understand what the Aussies at the other end of the line were saying and they similarly had difficulty understanding what he had to say. Srivatsa, Blossom's husband, made over 500 job applications for engineering assignments; only 20 of these resulted in a show of interest and just nine in telephonic interviews. He was happy to accept an assignment with a relatively small firm even if that involved moving to Adelaide. Cedric too struggled quite a bit and eventually settled for a job in the transport department, in what he referred to as the bottom of the rung, a far cry from his engineering qualifications and the years of experience he had at Carborundum Universal. Like almost everyone else he had absolutely no regrets in taking the plunge to migrate to Australia leaving behind a prospective career. Srivatsa too left a very good assignment at India Pistons to leap into the unknown against the advice of his senior managers and well-wishers who felt that he would not get any job in Australia commensurate with his qualifications and experience. Srivatsa isn't an Anglo-Indian but is so closely aligned to the community that you can easily mistake him for one.

It was very tough going for these intrepid migrants. At places where they worked, they had to cope with cultural differences and a certain amount of arrogant superiority from the Aussies. Rodney said, "I initially got a job in the Department of Health in an administrative position and had to pass a community services examination before the employment was confirmed. I faced a lot of curious questions about my English name and ability to speak good English and had to explain my Anglo-Indian background." For Rodney, this would have meant saying that his paternal great-grandfather was an Englishman. Generally, Rodney, like most other

Anglo-Indians, referred to themselves as Indians. "At every stage, I felt as if I was being observed closely for my ability to perform my duties correctly," he said. He felt he had to constantly prove he was as good if not better than the locals. Rodney added ruefully, "There were times during those early months that I felt I may have made a mistake and thought of returning to India." Albert MacDonald said, "I was one of the few non-whites where I worked, in those days, and always wondered what the whites were thinking of me." His son Craig, who migrated with Albert at the age of seven and is now 50 years old, added, "You can't always take it lying down. You have to give it back as you get it." There is an underlying racial streak in the Aussies; however, as Sheryl said, "The Australian government's policies on racial discrimination are very strict and employees are careful not to cross the line as they may get into serious trouble if reported."

For the early migrants, being treated as aliens must have been galling. No one speaks of the sense of disappointment they may have faced as they landed in the 'Promised Land' only to be treated on par with those bloomin' Indians. They would have hoped to find a congenial environment where they were well-accepted and free of the prejudices they faced back 'home.' Feedback from friends and relatives either spoke of a land of milk and honey or how tough it was and that it was better to stay behind. Aspirants didn't know what to make of these contradictions but migrated anyway.

Adjusting to cultural and sociological differences were not the only challenges that the Anglo-Indians faced and quickly adjusted to. Gillean and her sister took up jobs at a supermarket and had to travel by bus or train initially. Economic compulsions made them opt for overtime, working as late as 10 pm on most days, to earn money as quickly as possible; travel was a big constraint. "We bought a car in just about six months and I learnt how to drive." It would have been quite unthinkable for the Nash family to invest in a car when in Royapuram. The need to own a vehicle of their own would not have been pressing either. Owning a car in India in the sixties, seventies and even the eighties was a rarity. Errol said, "I bought a car and a house in just a year and a half after migrating to Australia. My dad and mom, in their lifetimes, were not able to do so in India." It was only in the mid-nineties, with the opening up of the automobile sector in India and the easy availability of auto loans, that owning cars became affordable and widespread. Professor Padaki, a revered teacher at the premier management institute I studied in, said, "In your days, students moved around in cycles. Some years later it was more common to find students commuting on motorcycles. Now you only see them driving around in cars." The material revolution has taken place even in India and though the quality of life that the Anglo-Indians experience in Australia is higher, opportunities for economic advancement have increased manyfold in India.

Battling it Out

Rodney and Gloria have a beautifully maintained house, down to the bathrooms which were spotlessly clean with toilet articles, towels and paper napkins meticulously placed. We talked about old times at length in the comfort of their living room. "The early days were a cultural shock for me. I was homesick and lonely," Rodney said. His cousins took him into the city a couple of times to help him get familiarised with the surroundings. He received quite a shock when his cousins suggested that he find another place to stay after he had spent just two weeks with them in Melbourne. "It was a dark moment for me and a time of despair. I never could understand why I was asked to find another place so quickly," he said, his eyes reflecting the sadness he felt at that time. He was out of the comfort and security of his home for the first time and was quite shaken. Luckily for him, Peter Pountney agreed that he could stay with him and his sister in their apartment in the western suburbs. "This was God sent as I now had the breathing space to settle down before moving to an independent apartment," Rodney said.

Fig 27. A quiet corner in Rodney's house

In his early days in Melbourne, Rodney felt alone and took decisions for change based on his instinct and gut. He said wistfully, "At the age of 22, I would have liked the counsel of family members or mentors but these were not available to me. A nagging doubt remained whether I was on the right track and whether my decision to move to Australia was the correct one. It was after almost a year that I felt more at ease and confident in my ability to integrate into the country." This was the most candid account of the hesitancy and uncertainty the early migrants would quite naturally have felt. The wine and the comfort we had talking to each other brought out this refreshing candour. Migrants of a later period had the reassuring presence of family and friends around them to smother feelings of anxiety; the herding instinct of the Anglos took many of them to places of work where others of their tribe existed.

"My educational qualifications from even a premier institution such as Loyola College in Chennai were not recognised in Melbourne," he said. "However, the company supported my efforts for skill enhancement by giving me time for studies and also repaying the expenses I incurred in course fees and books after I had successfully completed the course," he went on to say. He gradually rose to higher responsibilities in his company and went on to hold the critical position of a risk analyst. When his company decided to close its Melbourne office and shift to Perth, the location of its bauxite mines, Rodney chose to separate on an attractive package after having served the company for over 35 years. "For a while, I served the company as a consultant but needed to drive 100 km to the smelting plants at Geelong every day," he said. He would set off at the crack of dawn and return late in the evenings and it was getting a bit too much for him so he decided to let it go after six months. Rodney took the wise decision to retire in 2006 at the relatively young age of 57.

Now in his late sixties, Rodney and Gloria lead a rich and wonderful retired life. They have travelled around the globe on holidays and make it a point to go to a new destination every year. Gloria's interest in gardening keeps both of them busy tending to their garden and the grandchildren also take up a lot of their time. Such a wonderful time in the penultimate years of their lives is a just reward for lives well led and an affirmation of the correctness of their decision to migrate to Australia. As Rodney says, "This is a land of opportunities where dignity of labour exists and hierarchies are not so important. You call everyone by their first name and you can put your arm on your boss's shoulders. If you are willing to work hard, the sky is the limit."

The Indian migrant has proved his worth all over the world in spite of snide remarks about their accent. The Anglo-Indian is no different. They have by and large proved their worth in whatever jobs they have taken up. The quality of life is what strikes you the most. The Surraos, who are a large family of eight, are a striking example of benefitting from the enhanced quality of life. During the Second World War, their father Sylvester served with the British Army in the communications cell based in Iran. After the war, he re-joined the railways as a station master. He retired prematurely from the railways and settled down with the family in Royapuram.

"Those were very difficult days that the family passed through coping with the expenses and limited income," Cedric remembered. "It was only after Dad got a job with South India Flour Mills that the strain on the family eased, leading to more affluent times." The large-hearted Sylvester was quick to donate a cycle rickshaw to the rickshaw puller who used to ferry him to and fro from his home to place of work and did the same for the domestic staff.

The Surrao boys live comfortably and in far better circumstances than the crowded, though cosy, house they lived in on West Mada Church Street in Royapuram. Vivian lives in Brisbane, Cedric in Wantirna and Troy in Narre Warren while the other brothers live in Werribee. Alan and Keith live in adjacent houses, Godwin a few houses away and Geoffrey at a nearby street. It was most heart-warming to spend an evening with the Surraos and their family at Keith's spacious house.

Fig 28. The Surrao brothers

Troy says, "There is nothing like Royapuram; the friends, the warmth and the fun even if we as a family had very little." Yet it was with a great sense of excitement and anticipation that he set off for Australia along with his brothers Alan and Keith in 1987. He had completed a diploma in printing technology a year before but had not seriously tried for a job as he was cocksure he would make it to Australia. Cedric and Vivian were well-settled there and the brothers had a base to support them as they went about getting a job and finding their feet in an alien land.

Troy went initially to Brisbane to live with Vivian and Avril; he got a job in ten days while Keith took just three days. Troy found his feet in the printing industry and has remained there for almost 20 years. He said without any trace of bitterness, "I was retrenched from my first job but quickly got another." He switched jobs several times but never had trouble finding new ones. The benefit of being in trade is apparent. He is now well-settled in Narre Warren, a suburb of Melbourne, with his wife Wendy and their 14-year-old son.

The early days were tough as Troy recollected, "I felt lonely as they were very few Anglo-Indians in Brisbane and it was not easy getting socially connected with the Australians." There was a feeling of being inferior or 'backwards,' as Troy put it. Even at the workplace he often found that he was being singled out for reprimands and was the butt of jokes because of his accent and manner of speaking. All this changed over a period of time with increasing self-confidence and the ability to adjust to a different culture.

Troy went back to Royapuram on vacations almost every year initially but after his parents passed away and all the brothers eventually migrated to Australia he has not felt the need to go back. The Royapuram he lived in is no longer there. Nevertheless, he took his son on a visit in 2015 and showed him the place where the Surraos once lived and the old haunts in the by-lanes of Royapuram. Troy remembers, with a touch of gratitude, the struggles his dad and mom went through to enable all of them to establish themselves in life. The senior Surraos brought up the children with old-world values. Troy remembers the firmly ingrained values, "Respect your elders. Respect your brothers. Never quarrel among yourselves. If there are differences of opinion then respect the opinion of the older siblings and move on." He, like many other Anglo-Indians, is grateful to the Lord for all the comforts that have come their way.

Vivian, his wife Avril and their two little children Suzanne, aged four, and Dwayne, aged two, were sponsored by Avril's brother Desmond in 1982. He and several of Avril's family are based in Brisbane and so it is not surprising that Vivian chose to settle down in Brisbane unlike the rest of the Surraos who are in Melbourne. Vivian said with a great deal of conviction, "We were very clear in our minds that we wanted to migrate to Australia to secure a better future for our children. The living conditions in India were getting increasingly difficult and getting educational opportunities and jobs wasn't easy."

"It was a cultural shock," he said. "I missed the camaraderie in Royapuram where at six pm everyone came out of their homes and there was fun and banter through the evening with friends." In Brisbane, Vivian found everyone staying indoors as they returned from work. "Life was difficult as everything from cooking, washing and cleaning the house had to be done without any domestic staff for help," he said. Weekdays offered little free time and the only time to relax with family and friends was over the weekends. "We were sometimes at the receiving end of racist comments but in Australia, you need to work hard and if you are prepared to do so you will lead a good life. All of the Surraos have been able to settle in quickly," he said.

It took Vivian a couple of years to raise his standard of living but thereafter there was no looking back. He has consistently maintained a high quality of life. Vivian said. "I got a job initially as a factory worker but quickly rose to be a supervisor." When the company ran into trouble and its future was uncertain, he took up a job in the railways as a communication officer in the control centre. In 2014 he availed of a retirement package from the railways and is currently living a retired life albeit busy as he carries out his grandfatherly duties. Vivian willingly accepts that there were limits to his growth on the job as he did not have a university degree. But this did not worry him in any way. He is proud of his achievements and for making his dream of a better future for his children come true.

Vivian's son and daughter went on to complete university degrees in commerce and economics and Dwayne also completed a master's course in business administration. He is a

Six Sigma black belt holder and has a responsible position in the Health Department. Suzanne works for the National Seniors Services. Dwayne and his Australian wife visited India in 2007 and spent considerable time visiting Chennai, Bangalore, Goa, Mumbai and Delhi. Both of them came away from the visit with a favourable impression of the country in spite of the crowds, chaotic traffic, poverty and the dust and humidity.

A Beacon in the Corporate World

John Castelas exudes quiet confidence when he speaks and in an understated way, he depicts a life of success and fulfilment. John migrated to Australia at the age of 14 after he had completed his 10th class. He continued his education in Australia where he graduated in aviation engineering and went on to serve the aviation industry for his entire corporate life. He retired as the GM Maintenance of Qantas. "My wife Gita is not technically an Anglo-Indian. Her mother is and her father is not," he said. "Her father chose to leave a lucrative job as the marketing manager in ITC and risked it all to migrate to Australia. I am quite amazed at the risk-taking ability that the early migrants displayed," he added. John says his parents migrated in the mid-sixties because they believed that it would be good for their children. John says that whenever he faced the crossroads of life and had to make a choice as to which path to take he would reflect on the risks his parents and others like them had taken as early migrants and never hesitated to take the path less traversed. John's father was born and raised in Royapuram; his uncle was the nominee MLA in the Andhra Pradesh Assembly during Indira Gandhi's reign as prime minister of the country.

John has retired now and gets the occasional call for consultancy. "I am currently involved as an expert witness to the Federal Court on a patents and trademarks issue for aircraft tyres," he said. "I lecture part-time at Swinburne University in master's in aviation management and my subject is fleet planning, acquisition and contracts. It reflects the 40 years that I served in the aerospace industry, initially with Boeing and then Qantas Airlines," he went on to say. On the day we spoke to each other he had an appointment for a media event with the health minister as the first product of an earlier consultancy assignment, an emergency ambulance helicopter, was to be introduced into service.

"My real enjoyment is the volunteer work I do at the local hospital where I have been involved in establishing a Patient Health Information Centre which provides information from health peak bodies (Heart Foundation, Diabetes Australia, Cancer Council, etc.) and discourages the influence of Dr. Google," he said with a twinkle in his eye. In the midst of all his high-profile activities John tutors a couple of high school kids in English, mathematics and science subjects. He said with a laugh, "I get a rest for the next few months as they enter their Xmas break. But with Romeo and Juliet being their English text for next year, guess I will have to read and make notes as part of my summer homework." John has done exhaustive research on the establishment of Anglo-Indian education in South India by the Wesleyan Missionary Society.

Like Rodney and Gloria, John and Gita indulge in a fair bit of leisure travel. "We have just returned from a dream cruise covering Venice, Istanbul, Mykonos, Athens, Naples, Corsica, Nice, Florence and Rome. With a passing interest in history, this cruise coincided with the anniversary of the Battle of Trafalgar and I was able to read Lord Nelson's biography and plot his voyages in those parts," he said with the enthusiasm of one young at heart. Unstoppable now he went on to say, "The cruise before that was to South America starting in Los Angeles and going on to Rio via Cape Horn. The history connection was to retrace the Voyage of the Beagle, which was Charles Darwin's exploits in that part of the world, which sparked off the thoughts reflected in his *Origin of Species*."

In the Sporting Arena

It was still relatively warm in Melbourne late March 2016 when Rodney, John and I met at Rodney's golf club, the Box Hill golf club. We took a table that overlooked the golf range and the setting was just ideal as we sipped beer and talked about the Anglo-Indian experiences in Australia.

John said, "I am a cricket aficionado but I didn't know about Rex Spencer, an Anglo-Indian, till I read about him in the Guardian News a few weeks ago. Apparently, he played just one test match for Australia in Kolkata but the match was washed out and he got to bowl just five overs although he was considered a world-class leg-spinner." I confessed I hadn't heard of him either. He played during the 1964 series when Australia visited India under the captaincy of Bill Lawrie. Rex shot into prominence in 1963 when he was selected to play for Western Australia. His first match was against Victoria who were the reigning Sheffield Shield champion with several Australian test cricketers in their team. He created a sensation returning match figures of eight for 149 and South Australia won the match. Cricket enthusiasts talked of him as the leg-spinning successor to the great Richie Benaud.

Rodney had in the meanwhile quietly located the article in the Guardian News on his phone and read out snatches from it. "Sellers duly went on a wicket-taking spree and was soon described as the heir apparent to Australian leg-spin guru Richie Benaud. At the other end, bowling for South Australia was their West Indian import, Garfield Sobers, cricket's Swiss Army knife; able to bowl everything from wrist spin to pace. The Garfield and Rex show delivered South Australia its first Sheffield Shield title in 11 years with Sobers taking 51 and Sellers 48 first-class wickets, both more than any other Australian bowler for the season and for Sellers, at an average of 28 runs per wicket," he read out.

We sipped our beers in silence for a while before John said, "Rex Sellers' cricketing career was cut short at the age of 27 because of injury and a growth on his spinning finger and he retired from first-class cricket in 1967." The cricketing legend Don Bradman, who was then a selector for South Australia, and the team captain Les Favell were his mentors and supporters. Sellers gave back to the game by involving himself in club cricket, coaching at Kensington and also leading Adelaide to a premiership in 1975. He was a South Australian selector from 1979 until 1983 and after his mentor's death in 1987 he has chaired the Les Favell Foundation, which supports underprivileged youth in the Adelaide cricket community. Anglo-Indians often reach out to help the underprivileged; Kenny Powell, Air Marshal Keelor and others are outstanding examples.

Sellers was awarded life membership of the South Australian Cricket Association where he had served as vice president for 13 years. He also won the Order of Australia Medal in 2013 for his services to the game. It was time again for quiet contemplation as we reflected on the brilliance that had not been fortunate enough to rise to legendary status. As Rex Sellers himself said in his interview with the Guardian, "I'll never know if I was good enough to keep going at that level. It's unresolved."

Our discussion then shifted to hockey in which Anglo-Indians have played a key role in developing Australia into a world-beating hockey nation. Rodney said, "The early Anglo-Indian migrants in the sixties loved the game of hockey and established hockey clubs. One of the names I can remember was Charles Gaudoin who established the Harlequins hockey club in Perth." John added, "When the Indian hockey team played in the 1956 Olympics in

Melbourne, there were five Anglo-Indian players in the tournament. But only one was playing for India—captain Leslie Claudius; four, recent Anglo-Indian migrants from India, represented Australia." India went on to win the gold medal beating Pakistan 1.0. Australia just missed the semi-final berth as they lost in the qualifying play-off to Great Britain.

Rodney said, "Ric Charlesworth, the great Australian hockey player and coach, often acknowledges the contribution of the Anglo-Indians to Australian hockey as players and coaches. The Pearce brothers, Fred Browne, Merv Adams, Trevor Vanderputt, Don Smart, Terry Walsh and Paul Gaudoin are some of the prominent Anglo-Indians associated with the game." The mentorship of Vanderputt, Browne and Adams resulted in Western Australia becoming a hockey powerhouse. When the Anglo-Indian influence was at its peak, the state won the country's top championship eight times in nine years; from 1962 to 1970.

I was surprised to read that Chris Ciriello, who plays in the current Australian hockey team, is an Anglo-Indian. I don't member this being mentioned by any of the commentators even during the India Hockey League where he participates. Ciriello, whose mother was born in Kolkata, scored a hat-trick when Australia beat the Netherlands in the World Cup and also when Australia beat India in the final of the Commonwealth Games, both in 2014. Ciriello credits his grandfather Rudolph Pacheco, who was his first coach, for his basic skills. His grandfather played hockey in India before migrating to Australia.

There was an element of pride in the voices of Rodney and John as they talked about the Anglo-Indian contributions to Australian sports. We talked about other aspects of the Anglo-Indians in Australia. John said with regret, "The next generation is moving away from their roots and I do have concerns for the continuance of the Anglo-Indian identity. The various Anglo-Indian associations are a warring lot and never seem to be able to work together for the good of the community." Rodney does believe that there is a class distinction among the Anglo-Indians. This is largely on the basis of the economic and educational divide. He doesn't wish to join the Anglo-Indian associations in Melbourne because he considers it a divided house.

In the Twilight Year

Settling in an alien environment is a challenge for senior citizens. As Keith says, "They find it difficult to find their way around on their own, travelling by bus or trams. They find it intimidating. In India, Dad would just jump into a rickshaw and go wherever he wanted or just walk across to meet his friends. In the time he lived here, this is what he missed. The bonhomie with friends is also something he yearned for all the time." Many of the elderly, like Sylvester, chose to return to India. Gillean said with a touch of sadness, "My grandmother Doris Almeida struggled to adjust to the life in Australia and eventually faced a traumatic time at an old age home." Her emotions were understandable as it was in her grandmother's house in Royapuram that she recollects the best moments of her childhood and growing up years.

Doris migrated to Australia a few months before Gillean arrived in 1996 and lived with her daughter. Gillean recollected, "She was 70 years old and often felt lonely and nostalgic and would want to return to India every little while. She made several visits back to India but after some time she would miss the company of family members and want to return." In 2004 she had a fall and suffered a fracture. Her health deteriorated after that and she never went back to India. She took another fall when she was 90 years old and fractured her hip. "After her recovery and rehabilitation, she felt the need to move into an old age home," Gillean said with palpable unhappiness. "I cry from time to time when I think of those days," she said.

Gillean spoke with a lot of emotion of those trying times for Doris. "The care and services at the old age home were good but grandma felt extremely lonely in the company of aged Aussies," she said. She could not banter with them with her usual Tamil slang and found it difficult to adjust to their way of life or their food. Gillean added, "Over time she got used to the routine of eating, nursing care, physiotherapy, etc. but the loneliness and lack of company continued. She would spend most of the time watching TV in her room but later she stopped doing even this. It seemed that she had lost the will to live." Gillean and Bobby went to see her often and so did the rest of the family members. Gillean said, "I would make a drink of Milo for grandma each time we went so that she could get a little nourishment. In the last couple of months, she was unable to eat or even drink Milo." While in a semi-conscious state, Gillean and her cousins would talk to her of the happy days in Royapuram at PV Kovil Street and play her music of the sixties that Anglo-Indians of her generation loved to hear and sing so much. In December 2013 she passed away while in her sleep.

Fig 29. The indomitable Theresa Waples

On the flip side of old age care is Theresa Waples' experience. Theresa had a fall in January 2016 and spent time in the hospital getting a titanium ball and socket joint fitted. She followed this with a stint at Kingston Rehabilitation Centre where she spent three or four weeks getting physiotherapy and learning to care for herself. Far from being apprehensive and reclusive, she was fearless and confident at the age of 87. "Just a little wonky on my feet," she said. She has a sharp mind and vivid memories as she spoke to me of her youthful days in Royapuram in a conversation that lasted over two and a half hours. Her bright eyes, cheerful demeanour and vibrant voice set her apart from most people her age. Her regard and consideration for others were admirable. She well and truly bowled me over. To live alone in a two-room apartment is a choice she made and she clearly values living a life of dignity and living it to the full.

She spoke glowingly of the love and care she receives from the Council of Nobel Park where she lives in Australia. "The Council provides citizens with an opportunity to lead an independent life," she said. "We have a string of activities that include weekly visits to the library, walks with the walking club, hydrotherapy sessions and the movies." She added, "The seniors club also arranges visits to concerts and other places of entertainment. On one day of the week, the Council sends a person home to clean the place and help with purchasing groceries." A doctor also visits her home on a regular basis.

As Theresa said, "The government of Australia actively encourages senior citizens to lead a full and active life. What more can we ask for! If I was in India I would just be vegetating, whereas here I am happy and look forward to each day. I am very glad to be in this wonderful country."

Anglos in the 'Homeland'

There is more than a touch of curiosity among the Anglo-Indians I met in Australia about how those who remained have made out. The less informed believe that most of the unfortunates who remained behind have no option but to plod along and live predominantly in old age homes. The better informed know that it is a mixed bag with outstanding successes interspersed with the needy and the aged.

The Anglo-Indian community in India may not be as visible and unique as of old but they remain true to their values and lifestyle. They carry no complexes. They live and compete like everyone else and live with a great deal of dignity and pride. Here are a few exemplary Anglo-Indians across several walks of life, who will be a source of pride for Anglo-Indians in India or abroad and an eye-opener for those who have little association with the community.

In the Service of the Nation

Meeting Air Marshal Keelor was like a blind date. I didn't know what to expect, not even the nature of the venue at the basement of J-47, Lajpat Nagar 3; was it the Anglo-Indian Association office or what? It turned out to be the national office of Special

Olympics Bharat. Special Olympics is a movement started by Eunice Kennedy Shriver in 1968 for the year-round training of mentally challenged individuals through the medium of sports.

Fig 30. Denzil in his younger days

Special Olympics serves over 4.2 million athletes in programmes across 170 countries. Air Marshal Denzil Keelor is the CEO of this organisation which has over a million mentally challenged members registered for the development programmes in India. In addition, he is the chairman of organisations such as Literacy India, an NGO providing free education and vocational training to over 450 children and women from the backwards sections of society, and the Institute of Management Education. He is also the director of the Shanti Avedna Sadan, a hospice for terminally ill cancer patients. The Air Marshal says, with palpable lack of enthusiasm, "I am the president of the Anglo-Indian schools. The Association is unfortunately ridden with politics and factionalism. I don't care for such politics. The more affluent Anglo-Indians don't care to participate in the Association activities."

The Air Marshal comes across as a wonderful human being, unaffected by the awards and accolades he has received in a very distinguished career. He doesn't have the swagger associated with fighter pilots but that is understandable as he is now 83 years old. He says that it is perhaps time for him to call it a day but with the zest for life and youthful enthusiasm he continues to display, you know he speaks in jest. Friends tell me that when Denzil Keelor was the air attaché at the Indian Embassy in Paris, he helped the younger members of the team to settle down in a foreign land besides fighting for their rights for higher allowances. This spirit of taking care of the team's interests can be seen all over the Special Olympics Bharat office. There was an air of easy informality in the office.

It is this humane behaviour along with the basket of awards, outstanding valour displayed at wartime and the work that he is engaged in for the disadvantaged sections of society that make Air Marshal Keelor stand out as a very special person. He and his brother Trevor are well-known for their daredevilry in shooting down Pakistani F86 Sabre jets during the 1965 war, which earned for each of them the Vir Chakra. His gallantry spreads beyond this headline-grabbing action to sustained bravery and courage over and beyond the call of duty. On one occasion he lost the canopy of his MiG-21 aircraft exposing him to wind blasts and serious decompression. His ears, eyes and arms were severely damaged and abandoning the aircraft would have been justified. However, he chose to fly back the damaged aircraft and made a safe emergency landing at the air base in spite of having great difficulty controlling the aircraft.

Fig 31. Self and Air Vice Marshal Denzil Keelor

Denzil Keelor displays, with great pride, the citations mentioned along with each of his awards. One in particular that caught my eye was when he received the Param Vishisht Seva Medal for distinguished service. A passage in the citation reads, "His deep understanding of all facets of operations was apparent during the Sri Lanka operations. At very short notice he was able to plan and effect the massive air induction of IPKF (Indian Peace Keeping Force) men and their equipment into Sri Lanka, in addition to organising helicopter operations and accomplishing in time the reconnaissance tasks. The success of the Air Force operations and the swiftness with which it was carried out clearly indicates a high degree of dynamism, planning and dedication on the part of Air Vice Marshal Keelor."

Special Olympics Bharat, of which he is the CEO, has also brought him international recognition. In a star-studded event in October 2007, at the Shanghai Oriental Arts Centre, Special Olympics honoured 12 extraordinary individuals and the city of Shanghai for the special contributions they have made and continue to make in the cause of people with intellectual disabilities. He received the Special Spirit of China Award of Excellence along with world leaders Nelson Mandela, Arnold Schwarzenegger, Nadia Comaneci and other distinguished personalities. In 2016 he was selected by Sports Illustrated as Sports Manager of the year and received the award from Rahul Dravid.

In the 2013 Report of Special Olympics Bharat, Air Marshal Keelor writes, "I thought my 37 years in the Air Force gave me the experience of a lifetime. After 12 years with Special Olympics, I am not too sure about this now. My experience with Special Olympics has been enjoyable, exciting and challenging and construed by me as a big blessing and I am grateful to all who made this happen."

Air Marshal Keelor recollects the days when more than half the fighter pilots and trainers were Anglo-Indians. He says with a hint of pain, "Many left just after Independence and then many more in the seventies and eighties." He feels they really had no reason to leave the country. Those who remained and served the country well have gone on to acquire very high positions and even the leadership of services such as the Army, Navy and Air Force. "Those who remained by and large have no regrets," he says. I walked out of his basement office with a great deal of admiration for the man for his outstanding contribution and service to the nation.

A Gentleman Sprinter

Kenneth and Daphne Powell are one of the most dignified and pleasant couples you are likely to come across. Both were athletic champions in their younger days and their build and bearing while in their seventies still reflect the fitness and prowess of the past. I had the pleasure of meeting them at their small but tastefully furnished apartment on Lewis Road, Cooke Town, in Bangalore.

Kenneth Powell, or Kenny as he is affectionately called, was a gifted and highly talented sprinter in the sixties. He was often referred to as the gentleman sprinter; a title that suited him perfectly. He was the national champion in the 100 metres and 200 metres sprints for six consecutive years from 1963 to 1968. During this period, he won 19 gold medals in the sprints. A high point for him was at the East African meet in Nairobi in 1963 where he beat the reigning European champion Ron Jones of England in the 100 metres. He received the Arjuna Award in 1965. A mere record of his participation in international meets doesn't do justice to his athletic ability but for the records, he represented India in the 1964 Tokyo Olympics and at the 1966 Commonwealth Games and the 1970 Asian Games.

Kenny was an accomplished hockey and cricket player when he started his sporting career. It was only after he joined ITI (Indian Telephone Industries) in 1959 that the athletics coach of Rangers Athletic Club spotted his natural talent and advised him to participate in athletics in the sprint events. "I made that fateful decision on 31st July 1959," Kenny said. He immediately became the Karnataka State Champion in the sprint events. After a couple of quiet years at the National Games, he went on a winning spree in the sprint events in an unbroken run from 1963 to 1968.

If Kenny had been living in any of the developed countries, he would surely have been an Olympic champion. The facilities for training and coaching were in their infancy in India and way below the standards of world-class teams. Kenny recollected, "My day would start at 4.30 am when I would train and have breakfast before rushing to

Fig 32. Kenny in his sprinting days

ITI where work started at 6.15 am. At 2.30 pm, after work, I would head off again for training at the small playground of Annaswamy School just off Mosque Road. I would wait for the school bell to ring announcing the closing of the school for the day before commencing my training routines." It is hard to imagine a national champion training at such a playground which had a single track of 200 metres distance.

Kenny says, "In the early years I chose not to use starting blocks which cost me a podium finish at the '62 National Games.'" In subsequent years this situation of sparse training facilities would change for the better but they were still incomparable to the facilities that the athletes of developing countries had at their disposal. Kenny leaves it unsaid that if he had the advantage of facilities and coaching assistance that the athletes of the developed countries had he would have been a world champion. In those days the administration of the sport did not come directly under the Sports Ministry and funds for participation in international events or for availing of coaching facilities were extremely limited. The powers that be didn't consider the need to support sprinters who were often left out of the squad representing the country due to lack of funds. Kenny said in his usual mild manner, "On one occasion an athlete was left out to accommodate a cook!"

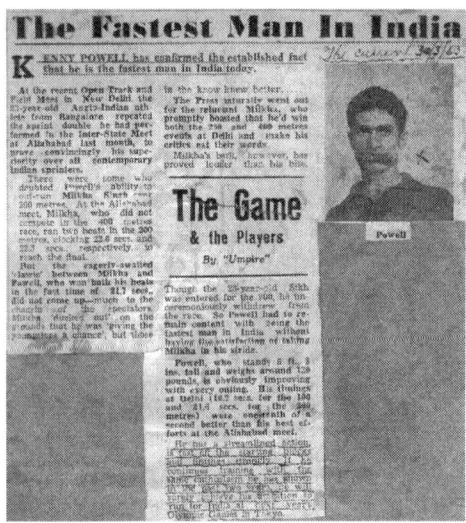

Fig 33. News clipping of Kenny Powell

Kenny speaks of the contribution of Anglo-Indians in the field of athletics. Derek Boosey, who was a champion triple jumper in 1961, migrated to the UK in 1965 and represented the UK at the 1968 Mexico Olympics. Derek went on to become the assistant coach for the UK Athletes Board before moving to Canada in 1970 where he was the chief coach for the Canadian team at the Montreal Olympic Games. In 1982 he was appointed as the technical director for the 1982 Commonwealth Games in Brisbane. Kenny says with a touch of resignation, "Years later, in September 2015, Derek Boosey was appointed by the Sports Authority of India as a high-performance coach. However, he was unhappy with the facilities offered to him and after a very short stint he left in December that year."

Athletes in those days could only represent the country if they or their employers paid 60% of the cost of participation. Kenny's raw talent ensured that he secured employment in public sector and private sector companies who promoted sports and sportsmen. AB Krishnaswamy, the then coach of Southern Railways Athletes, first got him a job with the Southern Railways. He later moved in 1966 to Tata Steel, another high-profile supporter of sportspersons. He stayed on with Tata Steel for 31 years till he availed of a voluntary retirement package.

When Kenny was a relatively unknown sprinter at the national level he had an interesting exchange with Milkha Singh, the Flying Sikh. Milkha decided to skip his favourite event, the 400 metres, and participate instead in the 200 metres. The standard of competition didn't seem very challenging for the Flying Sikh and he felt he would canter through to a win. However, on noting the timings clocked by Kenny in the heats and semi-finals Milkha felt it wise not to participate and face the embarrassment of defeat by a little-known sprinter. This is an exchange that Kenny remembers with relish; nevertheless, he considers Milkha Singh as the greatest athlete the country has ever produced and a constant source of inspiration as he sweated it out during training.

In the years after his retirement from competitive sports, Kenny moved out of the radar of the sports authorities in the country. His love for athletics and his desire to promote the sport and give back to society were very strong in him. Given the opportunity, he would have played an important part in developing young and promising athletes in the country. Instead, he was involved in various peripheral coaching assignments. For a while, he assisted the Special Olympics movement before moving to Sirus International, another platform for assisting disadvantaged people. These stints show his inherent compassion and desire to help underprivileged and disadvantaged people.

There is a strong streak of good in him that is very apparent even today as I spent an evening with the Powells. There's a spark in his voice as he speaks of his contribution as a member of the Anglo-Indian Association in Bangalore, where he was entrusted with the task of running sporting and entertainment events. The Association runs the triangular cricket tournament involving teams from Bangalore, Chennai and Hyderabad, besides the popular five and seven a side hockey and football tournaments. Kenny says with pride, "With sports in the Anglo-Indian blood, sporting events abound at all key days of the year such as Republic Day and Independence Day and are popular even today."

Two of Kenny's sisters migrated to the UK in 1961 after taking a torturous journey by sea via the Suez Canal. They threw themselves into the unknown because his son-in-law had secured a job in British Airways. His younger brother lives in Brisbane where he coached the under 12 team in the seventies and his younger sister lives in Bangalore. Kenny and Daphne look at you quizzically when you ask them if they ever thought of migrating. It was almost as if they were silently saying, "How could you ever suggest such a thing?" Both of them are very clear that India is their homeland and is the only place they have considered living in. Daphne, who was a little subdued for most of the evening, was distinctly animated as she said, "The love and warmth of the people around us is something that we will never give up." Such warmth she says is not seen in other countries.

Kenny's daughter lives in Melbourne and a son in Abu Dhabi while their youngest son lives with them in Cooke Town. Kenny has a brother who lives in KGF, who I understand has a treasure chest of information, documents and memorabilia relating to the history of

Fig 34. The family on a cushion

KGF. The Powells are a well-knit family and those living abroad visit India very regularly. The many photos that are on the walls of their home and even the photos on cushion covers display a happy and cheerful family. Kenny and Daphne celebrated their golden wedding anniversary on 9th June 2016 which was an occasion for a joyful family reunion. As I said goodbye to the Powells I couldn't help feeling that as a nation we did not utilise the services of a champion sprinter in far better ways to help coach and train budding athletes. Kenny now leads a relaxed retired life and is proud of his achievements as a world-class sprinter.

A Corporate Honcho

Gavin Standon is an Anglo-Indian corporate honcho. He is the director of Hewlett Packard Enterprise (HPE) Asia Pacific and Japan, managing presales for the business. Gavin wears his success comfortably on his shirtsleeves and is proud of his achievements. As he says, "You have to be among the top two in your profession to be counted."

Gavin and his wife Virginia live in a beautiful apartment in Cooke Town, Bangalore. Virginia has a calm and measured disposition and is a perfect foil for the exuberant Gavin. She used to work for Pertech Computers Ltd. (PCL) earlier but is now a homemaker and is busy with her social circle. "Well, there was no point in working once Gavin started earning enough for the two of us," she says. The Standons were originally from KGF. Gavin's grandfather fought in the First Word War and his father served as an attaché to the British Navy in the Second World War. Gavin adds, "I hope there won't be a World War Three."

Gavin's schooling was at St. Joseph's and St. Mary's in KGF, after which he graduated from RV College of Engineering, Bangalore in 1994. He initially worked in the bottling engineering line and was associated with the team that installed and commissioned the first high-speed canning and PET bottling lines in Pune, Maharashtra. He then studied business administration from IMT Ghaziabad and joined GE Capital, where he served from 2000–2004. During this period, he qualified as a Six Sigma master belt. In 2004 he joined Hewlett Packard and continues to serve the company with distinction.

Fig 35. Gavin Standon

A high point in Gavin's career in Hewlett-Packard (HP) was when he was selected in 2007 to move to the US in the Business Strategy Division for the consumer products business. He was in that role for four years during which time significant and far-reaching changes were made to the manner in which warranty costs were accounted. Gavin's credentials and his own self-worth were established during this period in the US. He developed the confidence to present his point of view and business case assessments not only to senior members of the HP team but also to high-profile customers.

So, didn't his successful stint in the US give Gavin a taste for like in the Western world, you may ask. Gavin categorically says, "I found the pace of work too slow. The opportunities for professional growth seemed limited. Outside of my professional space, I saw very little opportunity for social networking. Social networking is in the DNA of every Indian, isn't it? I am a green card holder but I was much happier to be back in my homeland. With all its quirks and problems, I love the place." This decisive thumbs up for living in their country of birth is something I have heard from all the Anglo-Indians I met.

Gavin has an interesting management student's perspective on the factors that led to the migration of the Anglo-Indians and conversely what has been the considerations for those who chose to stay behind. "It's a mixture of the circumstances in the sixties and seventies, economic considerations and career opportunities," says Gavin as he puts the issues into a neat little box. There are emotions and family as well as peer pressures too as I am sure Gavin will readily acknowledge.

"The situation in the country today has changed for the better," he says. Again, he uses the neat way of encapsulating the mood of the present-day Anglo-Indians. "It's all about ROB," he says. "R stands for the willingness to take risk; O is the perceived opportunities and B is the ability to take bold decisions. The younger generation in India today has a much greater appetite for risk-taking. They see opportunities for career and economic growth and are bold enough to go for it." The corporate honcho in him goes on to say,

"Companies in India offer a far more attractive value proposition to the young than those in the developed world. They are ready to take risks on what they see as potential in an individual and don't take a rulebook approach to running a company and managing its workforce. This is an attractive situation for bright and talented youth with a thirst for achieving success in life."

Gavin sees a winning fusion of the traditional open-mindedness of the Anglo-Indians and their willingness to imbibe the competitive nature of youth in India in general. The willingness to spread their wings and play to win is characteristic of the Anglo-Indian youth of today. They see opportunities in a wide sphere in the IT, banking, insurance, hospitality, mass communication and PR fields; they are equipping themselves to build careers in these spaces and are tasting success. This is a view that Keith Boye, the ex-principal of Frank Antony Public School in Bangalore, also shares. Keith says, "Anglo-Indian youth are going beyond college education to do specialised courses in hotel management, human resource management, etc. and also opting for B.Ed. and MEd degrees rather than the teachers training certificate of old."

Gavin says with a touch of disappointment, "The young Anglo-Indians in recent times are losing their sense of identity and pride in being Anglo-Indian." He feels that the Anglo-Indian Association at the national and state levels need to take this up as a cause and re-build this community pride. I would wholeheartedly second that sentiment.

Living Life to the Full

It was a tedious journey to Koramangala from Babusapalya; traffic was high in spite of it being a Saturday. The Byappanahalli railway crossing was closed for well over 15 minutes during which time two-wheelers, three-wheelers, cars and buses lined up on each side of the gate leading to a frustrating crawl to get away from the maze when the gates finally opened. We had a wonderful meeting with Bridget White Kumar which made the journey well worth the effort.

Bridget lives alone in a tastefully decorated and well-maintained house. The doorway had a beautiful cross signifying that we were entering a Catholic home, but inside there was only a simple altar at a corner of the drawing room, the only symbol of the Catholic faith. This was just as it was in her house in KGF as Bridget says, "In our house in KGF, the Altar of Sacred Heart of Jesus was fixed on the wall directly opposite the front door. It was strategically placed in this way so that the Sacred Heart could watch over our going out and in." She goes on to say, "We would always say a prayer and kiss the picture of the Sacred Heart whenever we entered the house or went out somewhere."

Bridget's house displays the trappings of a well-to-do house. Her husband Kumar had a penchant for collecting curios, many of which Bridget had to dispense with when she moved to this house after Kumar passed away quite suddenly of a heart attack four years ago. "He died in the saddle with a cigarette in one hand and the phone in the other," she said. There was just a trace of moistening of her eyes but she smiled through it and was determined to keep moving on with her life. She believes in living a full and regret-free life, giving full play to her talents. Quite unlike some homes which have survived for decades and house the last of the family, alone and forlorn, this was a vibrant house pulsating with life.

"Some Anglo-Indians who migrated to other countries believe that the Anglo-Indians who remained behind in India did so as they had no other option and lived in difficult circumstances, many in old aged homes. This is far from reality as many Anglo-Indians live well and the younger generation has competed in society and done well for themselves," she remarked. Her own daughter is an information security professional working for Siemens. She now works for Siemens in Singapore, has taken up Singapore citizenship and is married to a Mangalorian.

Even as it is increasingly difficult to come across the typical Anglo-Indian way of life these days, the small Anglo-Indian community in India retains strongly held and latent pride in their heritage. Though not openly stated they still believe in their superiority derived from their British lineage. Bridget says with a touch of pride, "Anglo-Indians always kept an open house. Their way of life was informal and homely. The values of generosity, hospitality and friendship were truly reflected in their welcome where there was always room for unexpected guests."

Bridget attended a wedding of a family member recently. Very much in keeping with the changing times, the groom, an Anglo-Indian, married an Estonian. It was, as she says, a typical Anglo-Indian wedding of the old that she enjoyed very much. She nostalgically recollects how much her late husband Kumar would have loved the fun and gaiety at the post-wedding celebrations. Bridget tells us that the Estonian bride, her family and friends were extremely surprised to participate in a church wedding in India, complete with the traditional wedding gowns. Such marriages across nationalities are something we are increasingly seeing with the Anglo-Indians who have migrated abroad. What we know as the Anglo-Indian community is quite quickly disappearing into anonymity but hopefully, the lifestyle that is so typically Anglo-Indian will remain.

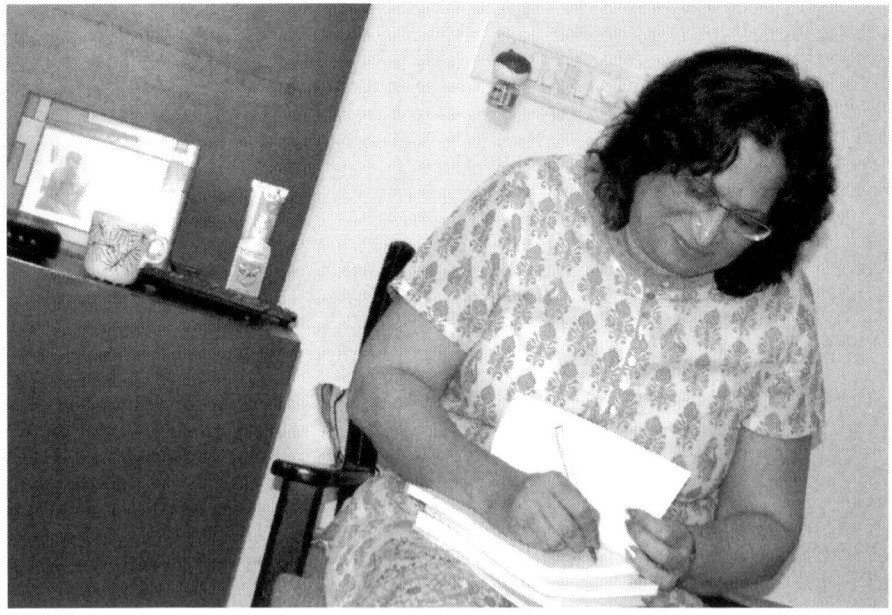

Fig 36. Bridget White Kumar

Bridget reminiscences of her youth in KGF and says, "Wedding receptions were always a homely joyous affair and everyone had a great time. Liquor was invariably served and the bar remained open until the end of the reception. The wedding march, the waltzes, the fox trots, the birdie dance, etc. had everyone joining in and tapping their feet to the music played by one of the local Anglo-Indian bands."

Bridget and Kumar were married way back in 1978, a time when marriage out of the community was considered a scandal by the Anglo-Indians. There was shock that she was marrying a Hindu. Even her parents disapproved of it and did not attend the civil wedding ceremony they had. However, two weeks later they had a change of heart and welcomed back the intrepid couple and conducted a Catholic ceremony at their church in the KGF. An early photo of Bridget and Kumar shows her with a large bindi! Bridget says, "You tend to bend over backwards to please in those days." Such inter-marriages involving the Anglo-Indian community are much more commonplace now. Even the church does not object, although clearance from the Bishop is still required.

Bridget is clear that she would never have migrated to Australia with all the compromises that would have been needed to lead a life there. She was not ready to sacrifice the dignity of her working life. Today, in her retirement, Bridget is giving full play to her passion for what she calls genuine Anglo-Indian cuisine. She is an author of several books on the subject and conducts cooking classes besides being called to guide several five-star hotel chains when they hold food festivals that include Anglo-Indian or more appropriately, Colonial cuisine. She has also authored a book, *Kolar Gold Fields – Down memory lane.*

Bridget, like many others, feels that many of the Anglo-Indians who have migrated tend to abandon their aged parents. They send money home but this is insufficient. The aged need companionship and care besides the money that goes for their maintenance at the old age homes. Community support seems to be the answer to this critical need. The Anglo-Indian Guild based in Bangalore, is doing a lot to support those in need, including support to institutions such as Friend in Need Society. It is good to see that there are sections of the community coming forward to help those in need.

Living with Flair Outside the Community

Gertrude Monica is an Anglo-Indian who married a Tamilian Christian, John Henry Ratnaraj, way back in 1950. Her father had only one stipulation and that was John Henry must convert to Catholicism, which he readily agreed to. John's father quietly and unannounced made a visit to Tuticorin, as Gertrude says, to check her out. He reported back to his family members, "She is a quiet girl and does not have the usual Anglo-Indian qualities." He was referring to the stereotype that Anglo-Indian girls tended to be vivacious and went out with boys. It's a stereotype Gertrude is very conscious of and ensured that her three daughters were all brought up with conservative values.

Gertrude is sprightly at 86 years and moves about without a hint of her age. She looks bright and cheerful and with an active mind; I would have placed her age as in the sixties. She misses her brother and sister who passed away leaving her as the only surviving member of the family yet her cheerful countenance brings out her zest for life.

In 1987 she made her maiden voyage outside India and was nervous and dependent on her husband. Now, several visits later and post the death of her husband in 1992, she makes the journey to the US every year to be with her children and grandchildren with the ease of a professional traveller. Her son and two daughters have migrated to the US and have married Americans. She now has 11 grandchildren, one of whom passed away after an unfortunate fall. Her daughter Linda married my classmate from St. Kevin's, Premkumar, and has remained in India. Linda and Prem never harboured any intention to migrate out of the country. They live in a well-maintained and beautiful house in the Vijaya Bank Layout, very near the IIM Bangalore campus on Bannerghatta Road.

Gertrude was just 18 years old when she got married. "I wasn't in love with him initially," she says with candour. "In those days when a boy proposes to you, you generally agree," she said. Her husband's family was very conservative but welcomed her and made her feel at home. She was the eldest daughter-in-law in a family of five brothers and five sisters. Being eager to please she took pains to adjust fully to the lifestyle of her new family. She ate whatever food was placed on the table and was loved by her in-laws. With her mother having passed away at a very young age, Gertrude's mother-in-law took over the mantle of a mother and helped her when she gave birth to her first two children in Tuticorin.

With John Henry working in the Post and Telegraphs in the wireless section, the Ratnarajs moved around on transfers, mostly to the secluded places where the wireless facilities of the P&T were usually located. It's not surprising, therefore, that she lost touch almost completely with the Anglo-Indian community. During her stay in Delhi, she often longed to meet fellow Anglo-Indians but never got to meet any. She had fully integrated with the lifestyle of her husband's family, even speaking Tamil with a degree of fluency not normal for Anglo-Indians of that time and dressing in a sari with her hair groomed in the traditional style. It would be difficult to think of her as an Anglo-Indian but for the trace of an Anglo-Indian accent.

I was happy to meet an atypical Anglo-Indian who made adjustments in her lifestyle as far back as the fifties. It must have called for an exceptionally strong will and family circumstances that respected diversity. Hats off to a wonderful lady.

Living a Life of Dignity

The gates of Eve Villa were locked. The beautiful cottage with its wooden triangular trellis frontage was just behind the old St. Michael's School music room in Burnacherry, a township in Kannur that was once predominantly Anglo-Indian. I had dragged Jayakumar along in the hope of meeting his class teacher of yesteryear, Ms Yvonne Gonzalves nee Correa. She was a hugely popular class teacher of standard six in St. Michael's School; fair, good looking and nicknamed 'Lip Stick' by the students, many of whom had a crush on her. We were just about to walk away when a sprightly lady peered at us from the doorway and walked to the gate to greet us. Jayakumar introduced himself as her student from the past and she willingly let us in.

She was affable as she welcomed us into her home and even took us around as she talked about the old days. Her open and trusting nature, even to apparent strangers, was refreshing. She didn't seem to remember Jayakumar but took his word that he was a past student. She is accustomed to meeting students from the past and welcomes them even if her own recollection of the worthies is a trifle vague. She clearly loved her days as a teacher at St. Michael's and proudly showed us the commemorative photo taken at her farewell party.

Fig 37. Yvonne Gonzalves at her home in Kannur

She lives with her son Lloyd, his Malayali wife and their two children. Her husband, a senior railway official, is no more and five of their seven children have migrated to Australia. A daughter lives in Bangalore. She loves looking after her grandchildren who keep her on her toes. Yvonne is a bright and cheerful 80-year-old who takes pride in being self-sufficient. As she says, her prayers are that she can walk and talk until the last days of her life. She lives comfortably on her pension and the generosity of her children who regularly send her money.

Yvonne has been to Melbourne, Australia on six or seven occasions in the past to meet her children and grandchildren. She enjoys her visits but always feels a tugging at her heartstrings that urges her to return. She remembers her husband and parents and wants to pay homage at their graves particularly on All Souls' Day. Besides, she says this is her home where she can live as she pleases and has been living here for the past 60 years. Fond memories are what she associates with Burnacherry. She tells us though that she is now trying to immigrate to Australia as she hopes that this way she can get her son Lloyd to be cleared for immigration. Lloyd does not have a steady job and is not employed currently. Like the Anglo-Indians of old, who have a means of sustenance, he seems to put little effort in finding and securing a full-time job. Yvonne hopes that employment opportunities may be more forthcoming in Australia. This seems a fond but misplaced hope.

Yvonne's clear and gentle eyes mist over as she speaks of her youngest son who died in a rail accident in Melbourne. She is convinced that it was an unhappy marriage and acrimonious legal battles that took a toll on him and led to his death. She points to a picture of a handsome young man smiling down at us and has clearly not yet come to terms with the loss. It is sad that he had to die in such tragic circumstances.

For most of our conversation, she was bright and cheerful. She remembers the old days when her house was converted into a dance floor. She took us to a hall just behind the living room where the furniture would be cleared to make way for the dancers. Many people, she tells us, learnt their first dance steps at this hall. Burnacherry or the anglicised name 'Burn Shire' houses the military cantonment and once was home to the majority of Anglo-Indians in Kannur. There are just a few Anglo-Indian families living there now.

The Gonzalves family lives the life of the typical Anglo-Indian families of the past. This is not a household that has moved with the times and adjusted to the changed circumstances. Their language, dress and habits haven't changed over the years even when changes have taken place all around. Their home, which Yvonne so graciously took us around to see, is typical of Anglo-Indian homes of the past. The walls are adorned with pictures of Christ, the holy cross and pictures of the family. There are photos of Yvonne at the time of her marriage and also one of her 25th wedding anniversary. The furniture is antique but the house carries a touch of warmth and simplicity.

Yvonne says she has all that she needs. The Holy Trinity Church is nearby and so is the post office. Auto rickshaws are available if she needs to go to town. The nuns and priests at the church know her well and take good care of her. One of her students, Dr. Venu, takes care of her health, including issues with varicose veins, surgery for her throat and hip and other ailments. He doesn't charge her anything for all her treatment. The services at the church once used to be only in English but in the recent past, she has had to fight hard to ensure that at least one service is conducted in English on Sundays.

All through our hour and a half long conversation, she was open-hearted, candid and not the least bit self-conscious of the house or its comfortable disarray or even her simple dress. She willingly posed for photographs and was smiling and cheerful all through our meeting. Her eyes were clear, warm and friendly. When we left her cottage, we came away with a feeling of great warmth for this lady who had dedicated her life to teaching young children and is now determined to lead a life of dignity till her last days.

A Touch of Zamindari

Patrick Kerr is the son of Lt. General Eric Kerr (Retd.). Born into a military family, he was influenced to a great extent by the military cantonments he grew up in and hence the fondness for adventure, sports and firearms. He was adjudged the best boxer in the lightweight category in the state of Haryana in 1980. His brother Michael chose a career as a shooting instructor in the US although he graduated at the top of his batch in psychology and earlier had established an excellent track record in foreign exchange brokerage! 'Follow your passion' is a creed the Kerr brothers have lived by.

Pat did his schooling at St. Georges Homes, Ketti and after pre-university at Loyola College, Chennai, he went on to graduate as a mechanical engineer from the YMCA Institute of Engineering, Faridabad. Pat had a chequered career, initially serving as sales and service engineer for engineering equipment and then getting into leather garment manufacturing and exports for several years. He and a group of friends then set up an adventure tourism company named Out There Adventurers. During this phase he and five friends set a world record for high altitude motorcycling when they covered four of the highest motorable passes in the world; Marsimik La, Khardung La, Tanglang La and Chang La in a non-stop ride of under 24 hours. The record was created on 1st August 2004 and is featured in the 2005 edition of the Limca Book of Records.

Thereafter, he worked for eight years with Hilton Worldwide India Operations, a high point in his career, before moving to Dehradun to set up the Carbery Acres Resort; a beautiful resort spread over five acres of dense mango and guava groves, once owned by the Carbery family and now owned by the Mann family descendants of the Powells. The land where the resort stands and several acres around it were granted to the Powell family by the Maharaja of Garhwal in recognition of their military services.

The monsoons had just set in and the weather forecast predicted cloudy rainy days with occasional thundershowers over the weekend that I was at Carbery Acres. The rainy weather added to the atmosphere and I enjoyed my stay. Pat is passionately engaged in the development, management and popularity of the resort. He has retained the natural settings of the forest resort and built a variety of dwelling units from Swiss tents, mud houses and a tree house. A couple of machans nested in sprawling mango trees offer quiet and unobtrusive observation of the myriad birds that can be heard all through the day.

Fig 38. Pat at the meditation circle

Not far from the tree house is a clearing surrounded by five trees, said to be the ideal place for meditation. A Reiki practitioner has helped create a spiritual zone or an energised sacred space with a circle of stones, the northern point having a red coloured stone and the southern point a white coloured one. The rest of the stones are arranged at every point of the hour. At the centre is a little platform for the spiritual guide. This is a popular retreat for quite a few visitors and the spiritually inclined groups to the resort.

Fig 39. The Tree House at Carbery Acres

Popular for the corporate off-site and team building meetings is an amphitheatre for motivational talks or cultural programmes. Built around a tree is an artistically designed bar not far from the structure that doubles up as the dining area or the dance floor or even a meeting room depending on what the visitors make of it. Bonfires and barbeques are also arranged when needed around this area.

The resort attracts schools from neighbouring areas of Uttarakhand for day picnics. Also popular are the weekend stays for children from schools in Delhi. Pat is in his element when he takes charge of the children as he arranges activities and games for them. There are rope and obstacle courses, sketching and painting classes and a splash pool for just a bit of fun. For all visitors to the resort, there are several activities that Pat arranges to suit varied interests. These include catch and throw angling, nature trail walks and the soon to be introduced shooting range where the visitors get a chance to fire a variety of firearms.

Pat's son Raul is a freelance journalist and scriptwriter while his daughter Amani is studying PR and corporate communication at St. Xavier's College, Mumbai. Amani, in true Anglo-Indian style, is a wonderful singer who performs at collegiate functions. Although his two sisters and brother have both migrated, his sisters to Melbourne and brother to the US, Pat never felt inclined to migrate. Pat believes that when you migrate out of the country you are invariably a second-class citizen. As he says, "Even today, at a railway station, a porter would call you sahib and offer to carry your luggage even if you had just a few hundred bucks in your pocket. You can never be a sahib abroad." He has spent several months in the UK and Australia and knows what he is talking about.

Pat does not show any signs of nostalgia for the good old days of the Anglo-Indians. His upbringing in military cantonments and boarding school is probably a reason for this. I wouldn't expect his children to be any different. In their childhood days, the community would have dropped well below the 'critical mass' and the cloistered Anglo-Indian lifestyle would more or less have disappeared. Clement Town, which was earmarked as an exclusive Anglo-Indian zone, gradually opened up to non-Anglo-Indian Christians and then was open to all. Pat says there are approximately 40 Anglo-Indian families still in Clement Town and the Sunday morning services at the church have a fairly high number of Anglo-Indians.

Pat's ex-wife, who divorced him by mutual consent in 2010, has remarried a non-Anglo-Indian. About the only expression of Anglo-Indian pride that Pat shared was his reference to nearly half of Mussoorie, in the days of the British and just after Independence, being owned by three Anglo-Indian families: the Hershies, the Skinners and the Powells.

The Large-Hearted Anglos

I met a former classmate, Clayton Fernandez, at the Friend in Need Society in Bangalore. I carried an impression that he was in a state of destitution and badly in need of assistance. I was quite surprised to see him well dressed and in a reasonably good frame of mind. I was quite clueless about what elderly care was all about and the distinction with care for the destitute. We were told by some of the trustees of the society that Clayton was one of the most helpful of the inmates, ever-ready to help others and going out on chores on their behalf. Errol Edmonds supports Clayton through monthly donations that take care of the payments to the Society and Clayton's sister Heather, who has migrated to Australia, also contributes towards taking care of his running expenses.

Anglo-Indians, by and large, are large-hearted. They never hesitate to share when called upon to help other needy Anglo-Indians. They are invariably good hosts and are very considerate of their guests. Those who have migrated to Australia, Canada and the UK have been generous in their donations, either individually or through individuals and organisations that raise funds, to support Anglo-Indians who may be going through difficult times back home.

Errol's support to Clayton is part of a fund, Education Scholarships/Help for the Needy Fund (ESHFTNF). Errol raises funds through various cultural activities in Australia and also through sponsorships for a walking pilgrimage to Velankani that he undertakes every year and has been doing so for the last eight years. In August 2016, I accompanied him on the walk to Velankani and saw first-hand the impact of his fundraising efforts. For the year 2016, 83 people made donations amounting to approximately A\$ 8000 as sponsorship for the walk. The scholarship, as its name suggests, provides assistance to Anglo-Indians for their education and also assistance to Clayton and others who need help.

Errol and I spent a night with the West family at Madhavaram on our way to Pallavaram, where we joined the rest of the group who were going on the pilgrimage to Velankani. Two young ladies of the West family, Susannah and Pinky, are recipients of assistance from the ESHFTNF fund. Susannah is studying chartered accountancy and Pinky, Bachelors of Business Administration. The two ladies richly deserve this support and I am quite sure that when they do graduate and commence their professional careers, they will change the fortunes of their family very significantly. The West family struggles to make ends meet with the father Gregory earning meagre amounts on daily wages and the mother Maria earning small sums through assisting the illiterate by filling forms at government offices. Her earnings on a good day would be about Rs 200 but there are several days when she makes little or nothing.

The house that the West family stays in at Madhavaram is due to generous support from a donor in Australia who paid the lease for a year. Prior to that, the family lived in very sparse accommodation that Errol tells me was completely unsuitable for the young girls. Seeing them in their relatively comfortable home in Madhavaram was heart-warming. Aid to the needy could not have been put to better use.

Errol's fundraising activities in Melbourne for the year 2015 included the Carols-by-Candle Light which was attended by 93 adults and 6 children. This event raised a nett sum of A$ 1480. The Christmas Eve (Family and Friends) Party had an attendance of 184 adults and 11 children with donations and collections amounting to a nett of A$ 4083. The New Year's Eve Dance had an attendance of 156 adults and 8 children with nett collections of A$ 3877. The 1980's Night Dance was attended by 126 adults and 13 children with nett collections of A$ 4000. The bulk of the amounts collected from these events were disbursed to the five charitable organisations across Southern India which include Hope for the Hopeless trust in Kilpauk, Chennai; Friend in Need Society, Poonamallee Road, Chennai; Little Sisters of the Poor, Chetpet, Chennai; Jeevodaya, Manali, Chennai and White Doves, Mangalore.

Errol has a most interesting background. He worked as a trainee engineer for about 16 months at a Swedish rehabilitation institute at Katpadi, near Chennai. This institution established a factory for manufacturing a wide variety of auto components manned by people with disability, largely those affected by non-infectious leprosy referred to as Hansen's disease. Errol was highly inspired by the people he saw at work at the factory. They were cheerful and hard-working despite their disability. It was an eye-opener for him and an experience that was to influence his future fundraising efforts for the disadvantaged sections of society. Ironically his next job was as a flight steward with Air India, a job that brought him into a more glamorous arena and an opportunity to see the world. He was acutely aware of the affluence in the developed countries he visited where most of the people lived in comfort. Errol was determined to play his part in helping the needy.

Errol is not the only one actively raising funds; there are several individuals and societies doing wonderful work in this regard. To name just a few, there is Basil Sellers, a businessman and philanthropist whose love for sports has resulted in major contributions to talented sportspersons in Australia and in the developing countries. Rodney Almeida, who has been engaged in fundraising activities in Australia for several decades and the old boys' associations of Campion High School and St. Bede's. The list can go on but the attempt here is to only capture the large-heartedness of the Anglo-Indians.

Basil Sellers was born in India and lived the early part of his life in the railway colony of the country before he migrated with his mother and brother to Australia in 1948. His father followed them a year later as he retained a secure job in India just in case the rest of the family wanted to return. Basil Sellers is known as the turnaround king. He has invested in several ailing companies and was instrumental in reviving their fortunes besides building his own wealth. He is an avid lover of sports and represented South Australia in the senior basketball league when the stateside won the Australian Championship in 1958. He provides generous donations to support scholarship funds for budding sportspersons. Some prominent cricketers he has sponsored include Phillip Hughes, Steven Smith, Usman Khawaja, Mitchell Star, Josh Hazlewood and Patrick Cummins. He is a patron of the LBW Trust which provides scholarships to 800 disadvantaged talented sportsmen in developing countries.

His philanthropy extends to India where he makes generous contributions towards education for slum-dwelling girl children. He is a leading donor of ANEW (Association for Non-Traditional Employment for Women), which is based in Chennai and provides vocational education for 800 persons annually and helps them find gainful employment.

Rodney Almeida immigrated to Melbourne in 1970 at the age of 21. An avid sportsman, Rodney founded the Cosmos Hockey Club, one of the best local teams of that time. In 1986, largely through his efforts, the Anglo-Indian Australasian Association of Victoria was formally instituted and incorporated. In 1992, with the help of a government grant, the Association established St. Joseph's hostel comprising of 16 single bedrooms, a common kitchen and dining and laundry facilities. In 1998 the Association successfully set up St. Mary's Retirement Village. (AITW: March-May 2015).

The Anglos In The Wind (AITW) very ably run by Harry MacLure, organises a fundraising activity every year to raise funds for supporting 42 less fortunate Anglo-Indians, predominantly seniors who are in need of assistance. The fundraising dance on October 2015, which was held in Melbourne and generously sponsored by resident Anglo-Indians, raised A$ 3600 for this worthy cause. (AITW: March-May 2016)

Desmond and Geraldine Holt had done outstanding work for several years in Royapuram and also when they migrated to Australia. The Anglo-Indian Fund Australia Inc., started in Adelaide, provided funds to needy Anglo-Indians for higher studies in Chennai and these funds were disbursed by a committee whose president was Dr. Beatrix DeSouza; Marius Menaud was the secretary and Desmond the treasurer. This lasted a few years and was a real help to some of the very disadvantaged children of the community. Gerry and Desmond were actively involved in the Friend in Need Society, Poonamallee High Road, Vepery for over 20 years, with Desmond serving on the committee and was also the treasurer for a period of time. They have helped many families in Royapuram, most of them studying in St Kevin's, with food and money. They even kept a girl student in their home so that she could get decent food and enough time to study for her final year exams.

Fig 40. Christmas hamper distribution at St. Kevin's school

Hope for the Hopeless Trust in Chennai was founded by a well-known Anglo-Indian couple from Royapuram, Milton and Patti Peters, who started off by helping a few homeless people with monthly provisions and giving them the comfort of cots, mattresses, pillows, etc. After their retirement, the Peters decided that they should do something for the poor and less fortunate, since they had the time as both their daughters were married and away from Chennai. They started in a small way to see how things would go and were surprised to find after a couple of years how well their initiatives were growing. In May 2009, Hope for the Hopeless Trust was formally registered. With their rapport and love for the underprivileged, this couple, today in their seventies, are truly inspirations for all people with their dedication and commitment.

Milton, affectionately called Bunny, and his wife Patti are a reticent couple not given to talking about themselves or the charitable work they are engaged in. Bunny is soft-spoken with an air of calmness and solidity about him. Patti has a spring in her step even at the age of 74 and a lilt to her voice. Both are strong members of the Votive Shrine Church near their house in Kilpauk and support and help at the home for aged care, Mercy Home, attached to the church. On their golden wedding anniversary in January 2017, the Peters provided a special treat of mutton biryani for all the inmates of the home. Patti gives spoken English classes for the children who join the convent and helps out at the day care crèche of the Home. Both being good singers, they are members of the church choir.

The Peters, like most Anglo-Indians, applied for immigration to Australia in 1977. However, that year, priority was given to certain categories of applicants and they were advised to apply again the following year. Destiny had a role to play as Bunny received a promotion and his career prospects were bright and so was Patti's career; there seemed no need to migrate. Their decision to stay back in the country appeared to have been ordained by the Lord's desire that they do his work in Chennai.

Hope for the Hopeless has two main planks of support; they provide provision bags for the poor and educational support for disadvantaged children. Patti says, "Many families in the slums are pushed into unfortunate circumstances where the mother is left to take care of the children by working as a housemaid or a daily wage labourer. The burden to fend for the family falls on her since there is minimal or no support from the father. Hope for the Hopeless seeks out such families and provides them with the necessary assistance. While we assist some families with basic provisions and medical assistance, we try our best to educate at least one child in a family." Bunny adds, "Educating underprivileged children is our priority and we are now able to help and sponsor over a 100 kids; some have graduated and are employed in managerial cadres."

As much of the work is aimed at families and children of slum areas such as those in TP Chatram, Rani Anna Nagar, etc. where family feuds are an everyday occurrence, their approaches to the chosen families can be tricky and arduous. Patti and her fellow trustee in Hope for the Hopeless, Mallika Michael, have faced many threatening situations. Undaunted Patti says, "We explain what we are doing and the rationale for picking families for providing assistance and this usually works. When we are sincere in our efforts to help we don't need to be afraid of anything."

Hope for the Hopeless has many heart-warming success stories. A bank manager once asked Bunny if he could help a daily wage worker who swept and swabbed the premises of the bank. When he and Patti went to visit her, they found she was living in a small hut and her son was sitting on the floor working on his school books. They decided to take him under their wing and assist him with school fees and even tuition at their home.

The boy was an eager learner and went on to graduate with a bachelor's degree in commerce. When he went for an interview for a job with a reputed financial institution, Patti instructed him on how to conduct himself at the campus interview while Bunny made sure that he wore the right attire. The boy got the job and now holds an executive position in the company. What is also heart-warming is that he has a strong sense of gratitude for the assistance he received and willingly helps out in the activities of the Trust, including assessing the plight of families who need help.

The Peters are emphatic that their support is for all communities and not restricted to Anglo-Indians. Many individuals and associations have asked them to be more supportive of needy Anglo-Indians and even withheld monetary support but this has not deterred them. "They are all equally children of God," is their strongly held view.

On special occasions, all the children they support are taken to a nearby restaurant where they order and eat whatever they want. These events are eagerly looked forward to as the children love the freedom to order the food of their choice. On festival days such as Diwali and Christmas, little hampers of gifts are prepared and distributed to the children. Bunny, Patti and the other trustees of Hope for the Hopeless work with their hearts and take several steps to see that loving care is provided for those whom they assist. In several cases, the relationship with those whom they assist endures long after they become self-supporting.

They share in the successes and major events of their lives such as marriages and the birth of children. Bunny and Patti have indeed provided hope for the hopeless.

All is not what it should be when one considers the utilisation of the funds so generously donated to meet the needs of individuals and families or to support charitable institutions. In some cases, I noticed that those fortunate to be supported seemed to sit back and make no effort to improve their lot in life. There has been an unfortunate tendency to take it easy and not strive for self-reliance. Many are put off by this attitude and are not enthusiastic about making any contribution to charitable causes.

At a quiet luncheon with Clayton and Raj Aranha, I was given to understand that there is room for improvement in the manner in which Friend in Need Society of Bangalore is being run. Aranha, who is a strident activist in seeking improvements in running the society, said that basic amenities such as a doctor on duty and a nurse, among other things, were not available. The efforts of Aranha and a few of the other inmates have led to changes and a gradual improvement in the facilities. There may well be two sides to a story such as this as is inevitable in such situations.

In the Footsteps of the Lord

It was around noon, on the 28th of August 2016, that the Pallavaram based Velankanni Walkers, which included Errol and me, entered the church of Our Lady of Good Health. The group of 90 followed the redoubtable flag bearer Gregory West as we marched into the church two by two singing, "*Vazhga Vazhga, Vazhga Mariye; Vazhga Vazhga, Vazhga Mariye.*" It was time for silent contemplation and prayers for our families and friends and thanksgiving for the good fortune that has been showered on us this far as we stood in front of the Altar. As we filed out of the church the members of the group hugged and kissed each other. It was a time to be grateful, joyful and triumphant after ten arduous days of walking the distance of approximately 350 km from Chennai to Velankanni.

Video footage and accounts of the pilgrimage that I saw prior to the pilgrimage indicated that most of the pilgrims, including the ones who have made the arduous walk several times, don't seem to prepare very much for the physical side of the effort. They leave themselves in the hands of Mother Mary, who they say guides them safely to her feet. Leaders of groups of pilgrims said that the power of the rosary was unbelievable. Whenever they were tired and exhausted or the weather was bad, they would recite the rosary and get renewed energy. I wasn't sure how I was going to manage.

Errol, my buddy for this pilgrimage, had done this journey for the last seven straight years and was my guide and companion. He told me that the experience of living life as the less fortunate of the society do and witnessing their simple yet pure faith has been the greatest motivator for his repeated pilgrimages. He said that I too would feel the urge to do the journey again once I have fully experienced it. We made sure that we avoided the ease and comfort that money could bring and roughed it out as the diehard pilgrims do.

This walk brought me shoulder to shoulder with several Anglo-Indians on a pilgrimage considered very special in the hearts of devout Anglo-Indian Catholics. I got the opportunity to get to know several Anglo-Indians and make new friends and appreciated how those who chose to remain in India adjusted to life in modern India. Besides I got to see first-hand Errol's philanthropic activities.

We started the walk from St. Xavier's church in Pallavaram after a special Mass for the walkers and the recitation of the rosary at the Grotto of Mother Mary. This is a walk of faith and consequently, on several of the ten-day journey the walk would start with the assembly of the group and the rosary would be recited and hymns sung as the group set off for the walk well before dawn at around three am. Shrill whistles by the coordinators would get us up by 2.30 am and everybody would spring up to get ready. As the column of pilgrims trudged along the road saying prayers and singing hymns I often thought of them as the Crusaders on the move. We tended to walk in sub-groups of four or five as the larger group split up after the morning rosary. Our sub-group included Elvis Smith, Peter and Philip Highmoor besides Errol and me. Along the way, we would bump into Dominic Ryan and his buddy Bhaskar, Gregory West, Neslon Joseph and Kevin D'Rozario. This was a wonderful bunch of Anglo-Indians I lived with all through this pilgrimage.

All through the journey, particularly as we crossed Pondicherry when the number of pilgrims on the road increased manifold, several people greeted us on the way with water, biscuits and tea/coffee. Just outside Pondicherry, a kindly soul served us exquisite cardamom tea. He told us he does this every year and generally serves 300 cups of tea. At Chitambur, en route from Maduranthakum, a family offered us lunch. They perform this service every year and started 15 years ago when there was no good restaurant nearby. Pilgrims generally pass this area on either side of noon on the 21st of August when the sun beats down on them relentlessly. The family started with just 20 to 25 lunches way back then but now serve up to 1500 lunches, all cooked at home and served by extended members of the family.

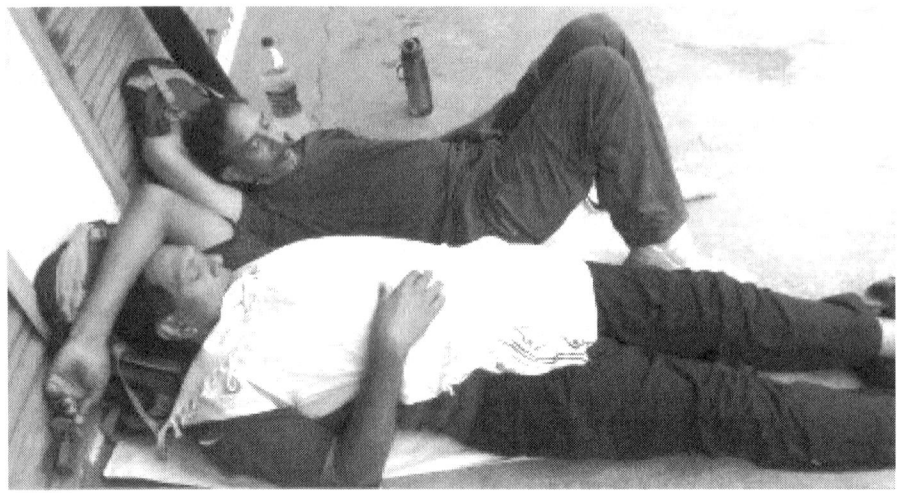

Fig 41. A quite siesta with Errol along the roadside

On a detour from Chunambedu to Koonimedu across the defunct prawn cultivation farms, we stopped along the road to have a bath at a pumping station that was pumping water into the nearby fields. The owner of the pump house and fields invited us into his house for a hot cup of coffee made from fresh cow's milk. At Cuddalore, the group stopped for lunch as they traditionally do at the home of the local MLA Sampath Kumar, a Brahmin, who allows the group to sprawl out on the floors of the rooms of his house to beat the scorching heat. His family members serve chilled lime juice and later in the afternoon lunch of khichdi and curd bath sponsored by Ananda Bhavan. In a display of multi-cultural support for the pilgrims, Rahim Khan, a Muslim, invited us into the compound of his house as we were walking between Erukkur and Sirkazhi. He spread out a polythene mat for us to rest a while and served cool and tasty water.

The heat and humidity took its toll as one of the members of our group collapsed with heatstroke on the way to Marakkanam. We saw at least one little child also suffer a heatstroke that caused panic among his parents and a desperate dash for help on a motorcycle passing by. Four years ago, our group suffered a fatal accident as a bus driver lost control of his vehicle and ran into the group. A friend of ours died on the spot and two others suffered critical injuries. Even on this walk, a motorcyclist hit a pilgrim necessitating medical attention for the unfortunate man. The heat and humidity make most walkers start the day at 2.30 am or so and walk during the cooler times of the day. Our toughest day was day eight (26th August) when we had to walk 48 km from Chidambaram to Thirukkadaiyur. It was necessary to walk through most of the day. Most of the walkers struggled on this day and reached halt late at night. Many tend to sleep or just relax at a shady spot along the road to take frequent respites from the blazing heat of the day.

Walking such long distances invariably brings the risk of blisters and everyone suffers to a lesser or greater extent. Those of us who took early action at the onset of blisters, to apply Band-Aids and bandages, got away with it relatively lightly. The others had to contend with a painful walk as they stumbled and limped along the way. It was amazing to see people of all ages and some with serious disabilities make the walk. In our group, we had an 83-year-old man, Mr. Varghese who walked on unmindful of an implanted pacemaker. He trudged along alone most of the time and successfully completed the walk. Our prayer leader, Rex Jacob, is 75 years old and this was his 43rd straight walk to Velankanni. He now flies down from Melbourne to Chennai along with a group of the faithful to join in the walk each year.

We could see amputees moving along on wheelchairs or hand driven vehicles and parents carrying their children or pushing them in prams. It was an enormous show of faith. Many groups had built floats in honour of Mother Mary and several pulled them along the way with ropes. The driving force was prayer and a plea to Mother Mary to protect them and lead them to her shrine.

Food along the walk was reasonable thanks to sponsors. Most of the time we eat khichdi or curd rice and idlies but on some occasions, we were treated to chicken biryani. On the first day, we had to sleep on the roadside at a spot between Tambaram and Chenglepet. We just spread out on the pavement unmindful of lorries and heavy vehicular traffic screeching by. It was the mosquitoes that were the biggest problem though. On other days we spent the night sprawled on the floor of halls at churches and schools and on the odd occasions at a modest lodge. There wasn't much creature comfort on this pilgrimage and it was never going to be so. Comparatively, our group was a lot better off than other pilgrims.

Fig 42. I share flag bearing duties

The walk was interspersed with religious events. Special Masses were conducted at St. Joseph's church, Chenglepet, St. Joseph's school hall at Nugambal, at the Villianur church and a convent at Bahur, besides the Mass at Velankanni. There are several activities that are heart-warming to witness and now a part of the regular programme of our group from year to year. At Villianur, which was not on the path to Velankanni but on a detour taken by the group, we spent time with the school children, most of them from broken homes, some of whom are financially supported by the group. The school children were provided with a sumptuous meal sponsored by the Walkers Association. At Bahur, the breakfast was provided for us by the principal and staff of the Catholic school. Further down the journey, at B. Mutlur, our sub-group stopped by a small juice bar along the road to have a cool drink of nannari sharbat.

We witnessed the flag hoisting signifying the commencement of the celebrations of Novena Masses leading up to the birthday of Mother Mary on 8th September. Velankanni is a sea of humanity on the 29th of August and is best avoided by those who are uncomfortable in heavy crowds. There were hours of pushing and tugging and jam-packed waiting. Luckily, Errol and I spent an extra day at Velankanni when the crowds had subsided and we could spend quality time at the church, submit our Mass intentions and pick up the candles, holy water, pictures of Mother Mary and the little things that our family and friends had asked us to pick up. Later that evening we took a bus to Nagapattinam and caught the night train to Chennai. That brought to a close a fabulous spiritual experience.

The walk to Velankani along with Errol and the Pallavaram Walkers Association helped me see at close quarters compassion at its best. Many had wads of ten rupee notes which they distributed all along the way to the poor and the destitute. The walkers never hesitated to offer a helping hand to others on the pilgrimage in need of water or medicines. Vivid in my memory is the assistance provided to the poor who had blistered feet and needed bandaging and medication. The spirit of sharing was also evident among the members of the group and so was the readiness to help with rail or bus tickets for fellow members who couldn't afford to pay for it themselves.

As the Sun Sets

I watched the sun setting over Royapuram and wondered if I would ever return. Some like Cedric say that they don't feel like visiting the place again, while some like Desmond feel a strong emotional urge to get back from time to time. They say that a fox never forgets the hill it was born on. I guess I will return and so will many of my friends.

Desmond and Gerry chose to celebrate their 40th wedding anniversary in Chennai. They renewed their marriage vows at a Mass conducted at St. Mary's Co-Cathedral adjacent to St. Mary's school. Later in the evening was a gala reception at Doveton Corrie's school. Several close friends and family members of the couple came down from Australia and other parts of the world, besides old friends living in Chennai. It was an Anglo-Indian event fully representative of the old days replete with a Grand Entrance and a Grand March. These age-old traditions, presumably from the Victorian era, continue to reflect Anglo-Indian customs and practices. With most of the participants being senior citizens there was a degree of sobriety in the event. Anglo-Indian pride came through strongly as aged couples shuffled along swaying to the rhythm of the music as they gamely participated in the Grand March. They are different, these people. They look different, act differently and speak differently. But these differences are superficial. When they are subdued, as they often are these days, you feel a tinge of remorse.

Fig 43. Desmond and Gerry at their 40th Wedding Anniversary in Chennai

Since the time I turned my back on the Anglo-Indians and went in search of a life and career of my own and my Anglo-Indian friends had resettled in a new homeland, much water, as the saying goes, has flown under the bridge. All of us in our own ways search for the meaning and purpose of life. The more fortunate ones hit upon it early enough to let the sunny rays of happiness into their lives. Others battle on in the quest for fame and fortune as well as visible material gains. Doubts and indecision about our potential and capabilities sometimes plague our consciousness diverting us from the path of simplicity and godliness to a path of anxiety and unfulfilled ambitions. A life devoid of complexity seems so hard to come by. Yet the Anglo-Indians instinctively lead such uncomplicated lives; that's the way I see how the lives of my Anglo-Indian friends panned out.

My life was wracked with anxiety and the thirst to succeed; perhaps it was more the need to be recognised as successful. The calming influence of Nichiren Buddhism made all the difference for me. In time the little things that lead to 'absolute' happiness gradually became clearer to me. In the Anglo-Indian way of life, I see many facets of such living.

I remember the discussion I had with Paul, Merlyn, Christa and Douglas during our meeting at the D'Souza's home, Perfect Peace, in Whitefield. Paul D'Souza remarked, "The Anglo-Indians lived life to the full. Living itself is a joy for them. They don't chase after power or position. Hierarchy is not a consideration for them more so when they hold senior positions in organisations." Anglo-Indians in senior positions usually adopt an open-door policy and have an easy informality in their leadership style.

There is talk of the lack of morality and lack of education among the Anglo-Indians of a couple of decades ago. Paul's mother Merlyn said, "Some people look down on the Anglo-Indians and say they don't have much up there." She went on to say, "When they stand before God he may well say that they have more than enough up there." Christa Moss, a German who married an Anglo-Indian and who has settled in Whitefield, added, "The understanding among many of what is good and what is bad is often suspect. The Anglo-Indians' open and transparent lifestyle and sincerity in friendship carry a lot of good." The informality and hospitality Anglo-Indians display impress Christa. They are gracious hosts, ever-ready to extend a hand in friendship.

My conversation with these long-standing residents of Whitefield perfectly encapsulates the Anglo-Indian mindset and approach to life. My thoughts raced back to younger days when the clutter in my mind kept me confused and despondent. I couldn't help thinking, "I knew it back then but couldn't say for sure. Now I can say quite emphatically that there is tremendous merit in the Anglo-Indian way of life." They are a hard-working people in spite of several examples to the contrary. The outstanding success stories of the community that were referred to earlier in this book show that their simple approach to life does not in any way diminish their will to be duty conscious performers.

The Anglo-Indians are not very visible these days in our country and not much is said or written about them but their spirit and way of life continue. When succeeding generations of the community yearn to understand their roots, as I pray they will, I know they will discover with pride the rich and fascinating traditions of their forefathers.

Printed in Great Britain
by Amazon

69487337R00118